REFORM OF THE CONSTITUTION

Other titles in The Reform Series

*

THE REFORM SERIES

Reform
of the Constitution

O. HOOD PHILLIPS, Q.C.

1970

CHATTO & WINDUS
CHARLES KNIGHT
LONDON

Chatto & Windus Ltd.,
Charles Knight & Co. Ltd.
London

*

Clarke, Irwin & Co. Ltd.
Toronto

SBN 7011 1640 4 (hardcover)
SBN 7011 1641 2 (paperback)

© O. Hood Phillips 1970

Printed in Great Britain by
R. & R. Clark Ltd.
Edinburgh

Contents

CONTENTS

CONTENTS

I

Does the Constitution Exist?

WHAT IS A CONSTITUTION?

A visitor to the Department of Archives in Washington, D.C., will find a document in a glass case backed by the stars and stripes and flanked by two armed service men. This is the federal Constitution of the United States, dating from 1787, the oldest written Constitution still working. It is quite a short document. What the visitor will not see are the thousands of cases decided by the Supreme Court on its interpretation since the early nineteenth century. A Constitution in the concrete sense is a special formally enacted document like that in the glass case in Washington, connected after a time by formally enacted amendments, though it may be much longer and fuller like the Indian Constitution of 1950. In this sense we shall look for the British Constitution in vain. The Constitution of a State in the abstract sense is the system of laws (statutes and probably judicial precedents), customs and often also conventions that regulate the structure of the State and the functions of its working parts. In the latter sense there must be a British Constitution, but its precise contents are often a matter of doubt and speculation.

Politics we are told is about power. The current language of political scientists refers largely to the question 'where does the power lie?', and the 'power' they talk about is mainly the power to make decisions. This may be a convenient analysis for the study of certain aspects of government, but from the legal point of view the emphasis is different. Constitutional law is concerned rather with authority. What person or body has authority to do this? By what authority was this done? 'Authority' is a more subtle and sophisticated concept than 'power', depending as it does not on mere force but on legitimacy or authorisation, that is, on one's being appointed, selected or elected and recognised as being the person who ought to do this or make that decision. The political scientist asks, 'Who makes this decision?' The constitutional lawyer asks, 'Who is entitled to decide and is obliged to accept responsibility for the decision?' The answers to the two questions, of course, overlap to a great extent at any particular time. Authority is supported by specific 'powers', rather than power in the abstract. We speak, for instance, of the 'powers', rather than the power, of the Home Secretary in relation to the police. Power is a fact. Law restricts power, and confers powers. Powers are specific, authentic and limited; and it is one of the cardinal principles of a democratic system like ours that a public official–anyone from a police constable to a Minister of the Crown–may be called upon to show in the Courts by what authority, or under what specific power, some damage to person or property is claimed to be justified.

Authority needs to be supported by powers, but the obverse is responsibility. Political theorists may be satisfied with finding the seat of power, but the lawyer is equally concerned with responsibility and duties. Authority is vested in a person for the benefit of society, and not for the benefit of that person himself. The concept of responsibility or duty is not only a legal one, limiting the exercise of powers, but it is a moral one reflected in the best traditions of public life in this country.

The word 'authority' is also used of the person or body in whom authority, in the sense mentioned, is vested. Thus we talk of public authorities, local authorities, police authorities and so on.

A Constitution, then, will specify the main State authorities–legislative, executive and judicial; how and by whom they are appointed, the relations between them, for example, between the Head of State and the Ministers and between the Ministers and the Legislature, and between both of these and the Courts. Nowadays it also commonly sets out the position of the individual in relation to the State. A Constitution, like the law generally, is also concerned with *how* things are done, such as the manner and form of legislation and the authentication of executive acts. A written Constitution will also prescribe the manner in which

2

these arrangements themselves may be changed, that is, constitutional amendments.

RIGID AND FLEXIBLE CONSTITUTIONS

If, as is usually the case, some special method for constitutional amendment is prescribed—for example, a special majority of (say) 66 per cent in one or both Houses of the Legislature, or approval at a referendum, or both—the Constitution is called 'rigid', and the provisions that cannot be amended by the ordinary legislative procedure are said to be 'entrenched'. Federal Constitutions are invariably rigid, at least as regards the distribution of powers between the federation and the constituent units. Rigidity is a matter of degree. Thus at one extreme no provision of the American Constitution can be amended except by one of the special procedures prescribed. At the other extreme the written Constitution of Singapore has no entrenched provisions at all. Commonly parts are entrenched, for example, monarchy or republic, and parts are not, for example, the number of seats in the elected Chamber. Very rarely, as with the 'basic articles' of the Cyprus Constitution of 1960, no lawful means of alteration are provided, so that any change (however peaceably brought about) would technically be a revolution.

The problem then arises, how to secure the validity of legislation under a rigid Constitution? The traditional method in other Commonwealth countries, and also in the United States, is 'judicial review' by the ordinary Courts. In other words, the Courts have jurisdiction in cases that come before them to declare that legislation is void as being contrary to the Constitution. The result may be that a citizen obtains damages or compensation for a tort (civil wrong) committed against him by a public official, or obtains a declaration that certain property of his is not liable to be compulsorily acquired for public purposes, or he is acquitted on some criminal charge. Some countries, for example, the West German Republic and Cyprus, prefer to vest this jurisdiction in special Constitutional Courts. For many lawyers in the civil law tradition it offends the doctrine of the separation of powers to

3

allow the judiciary to annul the work of the legislature. Thus there is no judicial review in France, but the Constitution of the Fifth French Republic established a Constitutional Council which examines proposed organic laws (laws not amounting to constitutional amendments but requiring alteration by a special procedure) before they are promulgated, to ensure that they do not conflict with the Constitution. Proposed ordinary laws may also be submitted to the Council by the President, the Prime Minister or the President of either Chamber. If a proposed law is declared by the Council to be unconstitutional, it cannot be promulgated or come into force.

BRITAIN'S ALMOST UNIQUE UNWRITTEN CONSTITUTION

Britain is almost unique in not having a written Constitution. In fact New Zealand appears to be the only other State at the present day in a similar position. Why is this so ? Most countries have made a new start in fairly recent times. It may have been the result of a revolution, for example, France in 1789 and several times since; of a war of independence, as in the case of the United States at about the same time; or the desire to form a federation, for example, the United States again, Canada in 1867 and Australia in 1900; or of a grant of independence to a former dependent territory, as happened with India, Pakistan and Ceylon in 1947 and more than twenty Commonwealth countries afterwards. No occasion of this kind has arisen in this country since 1066, a time when the customary feudal system rendered written Constitutions inappropriate, if we except Cromwell's shortlived Instrument of Government and the Bill of Rights of 1688, which dealt only with certain specific matters in issue at the time.

The State for international purposes is the United Kingdom, a name not familiar in our popular usage–for one thing it has no proper adjective–but conveniently referred to overseas as 'the U.K'. It consists of Great Britain (England and Wales with Scotland) and Northern Ireland. English people and foreigners often speak of the 'English Constitution'; although inaccurate and annoying to Scotsmen, this expression does reflect the long development of

4

constitutional ideas in the predominant partner, as does the use of the English language. In this book we shall usually refer to the 'British Constitution', letting this term cover Northern Ireland where appropriate.

SOURCES OF THE BRITISH CONSTITUTION

Our unwritten Constitution is the product of history, the result of centuries of trial and error. Where, then, are we to look for those principles that are usually called constitutional? The main sources are the same as for our law generally – namely, legislation or statute law; and common law, whether judicial precedents (case law) or custom. To these we must add constitutional conventions in order to understand how the Constitution actually works at the present day.

There is quite a considerable body of relevant statute law, parts of which would find a place in a written Constitution. Traditionally we begin with Magna Carta, drawn up by the Barons and assented to by King John in 1215 before the days of Parliament. Revised versions of Henry 3 (1235) and Edward 1 (1297), as imaginatively expounded by Coke in the seventeenth century, exercised a profound influence on our constitutional history, though in fact nearly all its provisions are now obsolete and have been repealed in the nineteenth and twentieth centuries. The famous declaration of liberties in chapter 29 (chapters 39 and 40 of 1215), however, still stands. The Bill of Rights, another revolutionary document, was passed after the flight of James 2 by a 'convention' Parliament that summoned the joint Sovereigns (William and Mary) instead of vice versa, but paradoxically it is regarded as having if anything rather more force than an ordinary statute. It did not attempt to be exhaustive, but dealt ad hoc with specific complaints about such matters as taxation, the meeting of Parliament and the keeping of a standing army. A few years later the Meeting of Parliament Act 1694 (still in force) provided that Parliament should meet at least once in three years. The Act of Settlement 1700, as adapted by the Acts of Union with Scotland and Ireland and amended at the abdication of Edward 8 in 1936, lays down the succession to the throne. The Union of England and Scotland which came into effect in 1707 rested on legislation passed by the Parliaments of England and Scotland, following the ratification of a treaty between them. Since James 6 of Scotland succeeded to the English throne as James 1 in 1603 there had been a Personal Union, but this did not have such extensive legal effects either at home or in international relations. The status of Northern Ireland, which has been part of the United Kingdom since the Union with Ireland in 1800, now rests on the Government of Ireland Act 1920, as amended in 1922 and subsequently.

The Parliamentary franchise and the conduct of elections are regulated by Representation of the People Acts, and nationality and citizenship by British Nationality Acts. The powers of the House of Lords with regard to legislation, the relations between the two Houses and the maximum life of Parliament are laid down in the Parliament Acts 1911 and 1949, both passed at times of political crisis, and there are later statutes dealing with the peerage. The Crown Proceedings Act 1947 allows civil actions to be brought against Government Departments. The system of superior Courts and the tenure of judicial office are contained in Judicature Acts and Appellate Jurisdiction Acts, and the Parliamentary Commissioner Act 1967 established the office of 'Ombudsman' to consider and report on complaints of bad administration, not amounting to illegality, on the part of government departments.

This legislation is sporadic and goes gack several centuries. The Parliamentary Commissioner Act, or any of the other Acts, could be repealed in the ordinary way. There are complications, however, with regard to the Union with Scotland, and we shall later question the validity of the 'Parliament Act 1949'.

The importance of the common law is a reflection of our largely uncodified legal system as well as of our unwritten Constitution. The existence of Parliament and its two Houses is a matter of common law. The House of Lords is the older body, having grown out of the feudal King's Council: representative ideas came later. The Houses were originally summoned, as they are still, by virtue of the royal prerogative. That prerogative, existing at common law, is the basis of the powers of the Crown, the foundation of the governmental or executive power. The limits of the prerogative have been defined by the Courts in a number of cases. Thus while it is for the Crown to accord recognition to foreign States, Sovereigns and Governments (*Duff Development Company* v. *Government of Kelantan,* 1924) and their diplomatic representatives (*Engelke* v. *Musmann,* 1928), the administration of justice is delegated to the Courts and the King himself could not give judgment (*Prohibitions del Roy,* 1607), nor has the Crown power to create offences by proclamation (*Case of Proclamations,* 1610).

The prerogative must always be exercised subject to statute, which may abridge or abolish it (*Attorney-General* v. *De Keyser's Royal Hotel Ltd.,* 1920). However, the Crown is not bound by a statute except by express words or necessary implication. Thus it was held that houses let by the Crown were not protected by the Rent Acts, and that vehicles driven by Crown servants were not subject to the speed limit, though the law on both these points was later modified by statute. It has been suggested that the presumption should be reversed, so that the Crown would be bound by Acts of Parliament unless it was expressly or impliedly exempted.

Our case law contains many decisions on the rights of individuals, whether citizens or aliens, in relation to public authorities. Among these are the 'general warrant' cases. In *Leach* v. *Money* (1765) it was held that a general warrant of arrest, that is, a warrant to seize a person or persons unnamed, was illegal and void. Similarly in *Wilkes* v. *Wood* (1763) it was held that a warrant to search for the author of a certain article, and to seize him together with his papers (unspecified), was illegal; nor, according to *Entick* v. *Carrington* (1765), does the common law recognise the defence of 'State necessity'. A person who is arrested without a warrant, in the exceptional cases where that is lawful, must be informed in intelligible language of the genuine reason for his arrest (*Christie* v. *Leachinsky,* 1947), and he must be taken before a Justice of the Peace (or, if the arrest is by a private individual, before a police officer) as soon as reasonably possible (*John Lewis & Co. Ltd.* v. *Tims,* 1952). Only the clearest express words in an Act of Parliament will be held to deprive a person of his right of access to the Courts (*Chester* v. *Bateson*, 1920). And if a person has a right, he must also have a remedy to vindicate it (*Ashby* v. *White*, 1704).

To the common law also we owe the institution of the jury, now used mainly in the trial of indictable offences. Although the jury has been important in tempering the law of seditious libel, its influence otherwise on the development of constitutional law has perhaps not been great. More important is the common law principle behind the remedy of *habeas corpus*, whose procedure is now regulated by statute, namely, that a person may not be detained in custody indefinitely without trial, but if he is not tried for some specific offence at the earliest practicable time the Court will not only award him damages but will actually order his release.

There is another body of common or customary law whose existence is recognised by the Courts, but which cannot be called 'judge-made'. This is Parliamentary privilege. The power of either House to commit people to prison for contempt, for example, was recognised by the Court in *Burdett* v. *Abbot* (1811) to be reasonable and necessary and well established by precedents. The Queen's Bench in the celebrated case of *Stockdale* v. *Hansard* (1839), while admitting that the Commons were the sole judge as to how a privilege should be exercised, asserted that it was for the Courts and not for the Commons to determine the existence of an alleged privilege – in that case the extension of immunity to the publication outside the House of a defamatory report. The Commons, on the other hand, have never accepted the principle laid down in *Stockdale* v. *Hansard*, and this is one of the debating grounds of our Constitution.

The customary part of our Constitution contains some of the most ancient offices of State, including those of the Lord Chancellor and the Secretaries of State, and the practice whereby most of the executive powers of government are exercised on behalf of the Queen by her Ministers.

The treaty-making power is an executive power vested in the Crown as part of the royal prerogative. Contrary to the position in some countries where treaties automatically become part of the national law and even taken precedence over the national law if they are at variance, treaties do not become part of English law. Treaties do not require Parliamentary approval unless they are expressly made subject to confirmation by Parliament, or they involve an alteration to English law as by imposing a tax or affecting private rights. The principles of International Law do not as a matter of constitutional law bind Parliament; but Parliament is in fact restrained by considerations of International Law, and the making of a treaty by the Crown may morally bind Parliament to pass any legislation needed to implement it. There is a presumption that Parliament does not intend to legislate contrary to the principles of International Law, but if it does so the only remedy is through diplomatic channels. Thus in *Mortensen* v. *Peters* (1906) Mortensen, an alien in command of a foreign ship, was convicted by a Scottish Court of infringing a Herring Fishery Act applying to Scotland, which forbad trawling in the Moray Firth even outside the three-mile limit. As a result of diplomatic representations the Crown remitted the fine, and Parliament shortly afterwards passed an Act providing that prosecutions were not to be brought for trawling outside the three-mile limit, but that fish caught by prohibited methods was not to be landed or sold in the United Kingdom.

Except in times of rare crisis the British have been disinclined to formulate their constitutional rules. Conventions, or rules of political practice regarded as binding but not having the nature of law, are not confined to countries with unwritten Constitutions, though there is naturally more room for conventions where the Constitution is not written than where it is. A great part of the working of our executive government rests on conventions, rules of political practice that have not yet crystallised, and may never crystallise, into law. The following are some of the most important examples: the Queen appoints as Prime Minister (an office created by convention) the leader of the majority in the House of Commons, appoints the other Ministers on the Prime Minister's advice, acts generally on the advice of her Ministers in the exercise of both prerogative and statutory powers, and will not withhold the royal assent from a Bill passed by both Houses of Parliament; the Prime Minister chooses the members of the Cabinet (an institution created by convention); Parliament must be summoned at least once a year; Ministers are collectively responsible to Parliament, and must either resign or ask for a dissolution if they lose the confidence of the House of Commons; it follows that a Government must resign if their party is defeated in a general election. How little the people at any time know in what direction they are going is illustrated by a provision of the Act of Settlement 1700, which was postponed and never in fact came into force, designed to exclude from the House of Commons all those–including Ministers–who held paid office under the Crown: whereas responsible Parliamentary government as we have come to know it involves the convention that Ministers *should* sit in Parliament, most of them in the Commons. The gradual development of democratic government since 1688 has been much helped by reliance on conventions, which are adaptable to changing ideas and circumstances. On the other hand conventions, such as those relating to the choice of Prime Minister and the dissolution of Parliament, tend to be imprecise, and this may lead to uncertainty in a crisis.

CONSTITUTIONAL MONARCHY

Such being the disparate sources of the British Constitution, it is not easy to describe its chief characteristics. We should begin by calling it a constitutional monarchy. There are distinct advantages in having a hereditary Head of State, even in a democratic political system where executive power is in practice wielded by Ministers, most of whom are elected members of the legislature. A peculiar glamour surrounds a hereditary monarch and royal family. The 'Sovereign', who ruled in the middle ages, now reigns as a national figure outside and above party politics and, especially in time of war and other crises, acts as a focus of national unity. Periodic presidential elections of disappointed statesmen, retired generals or dull nonentities whose names none can remember, are obviated. Even the expense of the monarchy is more apparent than real, for the amount of the 'civil list' voted by Parliament to the Sovereign at the beginning of each reign covers much in the way of salaries and upkeep of buildings, apart from the fact that the amount is considerably less than the hereditary revenues surrendered by the Sovereign to the Treasury. The Prince of Wales lives on the hereditary revenues of the Duchy of Cornwall, and gives half of this to the Treasury. The monarchy has also exercised an important function in helping to bind together the members of the Commonwealth (formerly the British Empire), especially those parts peopled by British settlers, although nowadays a Commonwealth country may be a republic recognising the Queen merely as 'Head of the Commonwealth' of which it is a member. An alteration in the succession to the throne, such as that which occurred on the abdication of Edward 8 in 1936, could raise difficult technical questions in the Commonwealth which it is not necessary to go into here.

Otherwise, the only reform overdue in this field is a revision of the Royal Marriages Act 1772. Under this statute, which was passed on the insistance of George 3, no descendant of George 2 (other than the issue of princesses married into foreign families) may marry without the Sovereign's consent: marriages by these persons without such consent are void, and all those taking part incur severe statutory penalties. However, a descendant of George 2 who is over 25 years of age may marry without the Sovereign's consent on giving twelve months' notice to the Privy Council, provided that no objection is taken by Parliament. It is possible that the exception of the issue of royal princesses married into foreign families exempts all, or nearly all, those who are in close succession to the throne at the present day.

LEGISLATIVE SUPREMACY OF PARLIAMENT

The primary characteristic of our Constitution is the legislative supremacy of Parliament. This means that Parliament can pass a law on any subject-matter, even of a fundamental constitutional nature, and can do so by the ordinary procedure of an Act of Parliament. Thus Parliament extended the maximum life of a

Parliament from three to seven years in 1715, and in 1911 reduced it to five years; Parliament settled the throne on the Hanoverians in 1700 and excluded Edward 8 and his issue in 1936; Parliament created the Union of Great Britain and Ireland in 1800, but dissolved this Union as regards the Irish Free State in 1922 while preserving it in a modified form for Northern Ireland; Parliament conferred extremely wide powers on the Government in both world wars, and in 1920 granted the Government peace-time emergency powers that are still available. This legally unlimited power of Parliament to make laws on any subject-matter is a corollary of the absence of 'entrenched' provisions and of the flexible nature of the British Constitution. It also follows that we have no strictly 'fundamental' rights. These are all different ways of saying the same thing. Recent judicial *dicta* will be found in *R. v. Jordan* (1967), where Jordan asked for legal aid to apply for *habeas corpus* on the ground that the Race Relations Act 1965, under which he had been convicted, was invalid as being a curtailment of freedom of speech, the Divisional Court stating that Parliament is supreme and the Courts have no power to question the validity of an Act of Parliament; and *Cheney* v. *Conn* (1968) where Mr. Justice Ungoed-Thomas held that a Finance Act fixing the standard rate of income tax prevailed over a Geneva Convention (ratified by the Crown) restricting the use of nuclear weapons, and what Parliament enacts cannot be unlawful.

Traditionally this is often called the 'sovereignty' of Parliament, but the term 'sovereignty' is best applied to a State in its international relations. There are theoretical difficulties in ascribing to Parliament sovereignty in the sense of absolutely unlimited lawmaking power. The (English) Act of Union with Scotland, based on a treaty and accompanied by reciprocal legislation by the Scottish Parliament, clearly expresses the intention that the Union should be permanent and that certain provisions relating to the Scottish Presbyterian church should remain unalterable for all time. The Statute of Westminster 1931, based on an agreed formulation of the conventions governing the relations between the United Kingdom and the 'Dominions' (now Canada, Australia and

New Zealand), expressed the intention that Parliament would not legislate for those countries without their request and consent, and in about twenty Independence Acts passed from 1947 onwards Parliament has disclaimed the power to legislate for the countries thereby granted independence. Membership of the European Economic Community or 'Common Market' is intended to be permanent: if Britain joined that would be an executive act, but legislation would be required allowing regulations, existing and future, issued by the Council and the Commission to be directly binding in this country as a kind of delegated legislation and to override any conflicting statute or case law. In all these instances the Act of Parliament concerned was passed, or would be passed, in consequence of an agreement with other countries (even if they only became independent as part of the agreement), which gives it something of an international character.

The Ireland Act 1949, s.1(2), declares that 'in no event will Northern Ireland or any part thereof cease to be part of His Majesty's dominions and of the United Kingdom without the consent of the Parliament of Northern Ireland'. This provision purports to prevent the United Kingdom Parliament from altering the constitutional status of Northern Ireland, or even from ceding a portion of its territory to the Republic of Ireland, without the consent of the Northern Ireland Parliament. It differs from the case where the other party to the agreement is, or has become, an independent country in that it does not effectively limit the powers of the United Kingdom Parliament, but no doubt it creates a strong moral obligation amounting to a constitutional convention. Although British courts must give effect without question to Acts of Parliament, there are international and moral factors inhibiting the exercise of Parliament's power in certain spheres.

This would not apply to an arrangement for the devolution of governmental powers to Scotland and Wales on the lines of Northern Ireland, though it would bear some analogy. Devolution to subordinate legislatures in England, Scotland and Wales has been mooted from time to time in the past, and Winston Churchill once advocated the restoration of the kingdom of Mercia. Whether devolution would be desirable, and (if so) what form it should take, are questions that fall outside the scope of this book; but it is difficult to see how any form of devolution would be practicable without some regional taxing power, which raises a big problem.

Some writers express the opinion that Parliament can limit itself as to the 'manner and form' of legislation, for example, by prescribing that statutes dealing with specified matters shall require the support of a larger than simple majority in either or both Houses (for example, 66 per cent) or the approval of the majority of voters at a referendum. The view expressed in chapter 7 is that this argument is mistaken, that English Courts need only satisfy themselves that the statute concerned *is* an Act of Parliament, and that restrictions on manner and form—as on subject-matter—could only be imposed on Parliament by some 'higher law' which does not at present exist. In earlier times there were occasional judicial *dicta* to the effect that an Act of Parliament contrary to reason would be void, notably *Dr. Bonham's Case* (1610), but although they helped American constitutionalists to develop the doctrine of a 'higher law' that could override even Acts of Congress, nothing came of the idea in this country and it failed to survive the alliance of Parliament with the lawyers at the Revolution. The higher law restricting the law-making power of most legislatures, with regard to either subject-matter or procedure, is the written Constitution which, so far from being an enactment of the legislature, created the legislature itself.

REPRESENTATIVE AND RESPONSIBLE PARLIAMENTARY GOVERNMENT

Parliament is a large deliberative and legislative body. It does not govern, has never tried to govern (except for a revolutionary period in the seventeenth century), and could not govern. Nevertheless our political system is often described as Parliamentary government. This expresses the idea that the Houses of Parliament, especially the Commons, claim the right to supervise every aspect of the administration. The government of the country is carried on by Ministers who sit in Parliament, and it is carried on through Parliament in the sense that Ministers submit their policies to the Houses for approval, they rely on Parliament to pass any laws that may be necessary to implement those policies, and they answer questions in the House concerning matters dealt with by their departments.

'Responsible government' implies that Ministers are collectively and individually answerable to Parliament, and depend on the confidence of the House of Commons for their retention of office. This is a matter of convention. It is in marked contrast to the American type of Presidential system, where the President (in whom the executive power of the State is vested) is not a member of Congress but holds office for a fixed term of four years regardless of whether he can command a majority in either House.

Responsible government involves representative government. Its existence implies that the legislature in and through whom Ministers govern is representative, or at least contains one representative chamber whose confidence they must retain. Although Parliament traces its history back to the thirteenth century, it is only within the last hundred years that universal adult suffrage and the secret ballot have made representation of the people genuine. Free elections with a free choice of candidates lead to the formation of political parties. Our present system of Parliamentary government, with a one-party Cabinet and an Opposition prepared to take over the administration, depends as a fact on political parties. The law is not much concerned with them except that it provides salaries for the Leaders of the Opposition in both Houses, and regards parties as lawful so long as their aims or methods are not unlawful, which they would be if they advocated the overthrow of our public institutions by violent means.

Representation is not exact. Constituencies are not intended to be numerically equal regardless of other factors. On a population basis Scotland and Wales are over-represented, and Northern Ireland (which also has its own Parliament) is under-represented at Westminster. The Liberals as a party are under-represented. The theory that single-member constituencies enable candidates and electors, or members and constituents, to know one another must now be illusory; but it would be against the interest of the two main parties to introduce proportional representation. A system of single transferable vote would help the third party. On the other hand, the regulated inequality of our present system does usually enable us to have periods of strong government, and it does preserve us from a multiplicity of small parties jockeying for position in a series of coalitions such as are seen on the continent.

INDEPENDENCE OF THE JUDICIARY

The independence of the judges of the superior Courts from interference or intimidation by the Government is a cardinal feature of our constitutional law. It was not based on any theory of the separation of powers, but was enacted in the Act of Settlement 1700 (since repealed in this respect and re-enacted) as a result of the malpractices of the later Stuarts. Custom also impels the Houses of Parliament to show considerable restraint in criticising the activities of the Courts. The principle of judicial independence is not infringed by the fact that judges are appointed by the Executive, that is, on the recommendation of the Prime Minister after consulting the Lord Chancellor, for they have to be appointed by someone. The question whether our actual method of securing judicial independence is satisfactory is discussed in chapter 5.

As a number of criticisms of our Constitution are made in this book, it would be as well if before going any further we paid tribute to its outstanding merits. In addition to our constitutional Monarchy, chief among these merits are the impartial administration of justice by fearless and incorruptible judges; the existence of effective remedies for the vindication of rights, most notably *habeas corpus*; and the principle that the members of the Government themselves are subject to law and that, though they may be able to show that their actions are justified by special legal powers, they cannot simply rely on the defence of 'State necessity'. But all these principles subsist on sufferance and are at the mercy of the legislative supremacy of Parliament.

IMPORTANT AREAS OF UNCERTAINTY

Hitherto admirers of the British Constitution would have added flexibility, freedom to develop, as one of its leading virtues. We ought now to ask ourselves whether it is not too malleable. There are important areas of uncertainty in the statute law, the common law and the conventions. This lack of precision, combined with extreme flexibility, may render the Constitution precarious.

As examples of the uncertain effect of some of the basic statutes let us take those governing the union between England and Scotland and the relations between the two Houses of Parliament. The treaty and the associated legislation, by which the Parliament of Great Britain was brought into being as the successor of the Parliaments of England and Scotland, contain some clauses that reserve to the British Parliament powers of subsequent modification, and other clauses that either express no such power or emphatically declare that the provision shall be fundamental and unalterable in all time coming. Scots private law, although alterable by the Parliament of Great Britain, was not to be altered 'except for evident utility of the subjects within Scotland'. Who has power to decide whether such alteration is for the evident utility of Scottish citizens: Parliament before the Bill is passed, or the Scottish Courts afterwards? Presumably everyone is happy if the Bill satisfies the Scottish Grand Committee, the majority of which consists of all the members who represent Scottish constituencies. More important is the question whether Parliament has power to repeal the provisions confirming the establishment of the Protestant and Presbyterian government in Scotland as a 'fundamental and essential condition' of the Union 'for ever'. English constitutional lawyers assume that the Parliament of Great Britain inherited the 'sovereignty' of the English Parliament and so, although morally bound by the terms of the Union, it could legally repudiate them. In a case in the Scottish Courts (*McCormick* v. *Lord Advocate*, 1953), however, judicial doubt was thrown on this opinion. The Rector of Glasgow University and a law student, who were chairman and honorary secretary of the Scottish Covenant

Association, asked the Court to prevent Ministers and officers of State from using the royal title 'Elizabeth the Second' in Scotland, as it was not only contrary to historical fact but in contravention of the Treaty of Union. The Court of Session held that the Treaty had nothing to do with the royal title, the proclamation of which was an executive act, and this was enough to dispose of the case. Further, the petitioners had no interest legally entitling them to sue, so anything the Court said about the legislative power of Parliament was doubly *obiter*. However, the Lord President (Lord Cooper) went on to say that he was not satisfied that Parliament could lawfully override these provisions of the Treaty (or Act) of Union, though he weakened his statement by adding that the Court would have no jurisdiction to entertain the issue.

If Parliament infringed the 'fundamental law' of the Union, it could hardly be said that the Union would be terminated for England and Scotland are no longer separately identifiable nations. Nor would the question be within the competence of the International Court of Justice, as has been suggested. Suppose the time came when the Presbyterian church ceased to be a majority church in Scotland. How would the wishes of the Scottish people be known? The members of Parliament for Scottish constituencies are in a minority in the Commons and are not necessarily Scotsmen. There was no provision in the Treaty (which technically ceased to exist at the Union) for appointing commissioners to negotiate a revision, or for holding a plebiscite in Scotland. The opinion of some Scottish constitutional lawyers, if pressed to its conclusion, therefore, would mean that there would be no way of making the desired change except by what would technically be a revolution.

The problem of the Parliament Acts is discussed more fully in chapter 4. Here we may put the matter simply in this way. The Parliament Act 1911, to which the House of Lords (however reluctantly) consented, conferred on the Sovereign and the House of Commons the power in certain clearly defined conditions to turn a public Bill into an Act of Parliament although the Lords had declined to consent to it. In 1949 the royal assent was given to a Parliament Bill the purpose of which was to reduce still further the period during which the Lords might delay a public Bill other than a Money Bill. But this 'Parliament Act 1949' did not receive the consent of the House of Lords, and so it offends the general principle both of logic and law that a delegate (such as the Queen and Commons acting under the provisions of the Parliament Act 1911 would be) cannot alter the terms under which his authority is delegated. So far no 'Act' has been passed without the consent of the House of Lords under the provisions of the 'Parliament Act 1949', and it is to be hoped that the whole matter of the composition and powers of the Second Chamber will have been satisfactorily settled before we get any 'Acts' depending in the doubtful basis of that of 1949.

The uncertainty of the royal prerogative or common law powers of government may be illustrated by the *Burmah Oil Company's Case* which puzzled and divided the Law Lords in 1965. When the Japanese in 1942 invaded Burma, which was then a British Colony, the British commanding officer ordered the destruction of the Burmah Oil Company's oil installations to prevent them falling into the hands of the advancing enemy. After years of negotiations the company brought proceedings in Scotland claiming compensation from the Crown. The House of Lords on appeal held by a majority of three to two that, although compensation had never been payable at common law for 'battle' damage, or damage (whether deliberate or accidental) done actually in battle, this was 'denial' damage–a form of economic warfare–and there was no general rule that such a prerogative can be exercised without paying compensation. Lord Reid, a distinguished constitutional lawyer, who was in the majority, said that as there was no precedent of such compensation not being paid, it was payable. The majority judgments did not tell us, however, by what method or on what basis compensation would be assessed, nor by what common law procedure (such as petitition of right before that remedy was abolished by the Crown Proceedings Act 1947) compensation could have been claimed in former times. Lord Radcliffe, another distinguished constitutional lawyer, dissenting said, with logic equal to Lord Reid's, that as there was no precedent of such a claim being paid, it was not payable. Since the prerogative was so vague and uncertain he preferred to base his opinion on the idea of necessity: the Crown had as much a duty as a right to do what it did, and it was not a source of profit to the Crown.

Now the decision that the Government was liable to pay compensation amounting to anything from a nominal sum to £100,000,000, came as a blow to the Chancellor of the Exchequer, whose predecessors in office had years before set aside as much money as they thought fair for compensation for war damage overseas, from which the Burmah Oil Company itself had benefited. Also the policy was that compensation for all war damage, whether at home or abroad, should be authorised by Act of Parliament within the limits the nation could afford. Therefore as a result of this case Parliament passed the War Damage Act 1965 (which had been prepared by the previous Government, now the Opposition) nullifying the decision of the House of Lords by abolishing retrospectively any right which the citizen may have had at common law to compensation from the Crown in such cases.

Incidentally, this illustrates the power of Parliament to legislate with retroactive effect. Lawyers in both Houses strongly objected to this aspect of the Bill, but there were certainly extenuating circumstances, and in any event the objection to retrospective legislation (prohibited by the American Constitution) applies mainly to penal laws.

Constitutional conventions inevitably tend to be imprecise, and so it is no surprise that some of our conventions also have an element of uncertainty. Examples are the Sovereign's choice of a successor to a Prime Minister who dies in office or resigns for personal, as distinct from political, reasons; and the circumstances (if any) in which the Queen might dismiss her Ministers (for example, if they introduced a policy of gerrymandering the constituencies) or might refuse a request for a dissolution (for example, if a Government had been returned with a small majority in the House after two general elections at short intervals).

So there is our Constitution, with no entrenched provisions, no fundamental rights and no judicial review of legislation. What with the flexibility of the law and the uncertainty of the conventions, an enormous amount of *de facto* power has come to be concentrated in the hands of the Prime Minister of the day–too much power, we may think, for one man. Does the Leviathan turn out on closer inspection to be a spineless monster floating with the tide?

2

The Government

The Sovereign as Head of State performs certain official acts in person. Ministers go to Buckingham Palace to kiss hands on appointment and to take leave on their resignation. Where there are seals of office, the Queen hands them over and takes them back. She receives their credentials from foreign ambassadors. She opens Parliament and reads the Queen's Speech (drafted by the Cabinet), though this may be done by commission. She can attend to give the royal assent to Bills or to dissolve Parliament, but these are invariably now done by commission. She presides over the Privy Council–a harmless survival that has its uses–and assents formally to Orders in Council. She signs innumerable warrants and commissions. It is commonly but erroneously believed that the Queen is 'head' of the Church of England (a title assumed by Henry 8 for a time), and that the bishops pay homage to her in that capacity; whereas in fact she is titular 'Governor' of that Church, and the bishops pay homage in respect of their episcopal lands. The Queen distributes the insignia of honours that have been awarded. She personally chooses the recipients of certain honours, namely, the Order of Merit, the Orders of the Garter, the Thistle and St. Patrick, and the Royal Victoria Order. Thus in November 1965 after U.D.I. she made the Governor of Rhodesia a K.C.V.O. Although peerages are created on the advice of the Prime Minister, George 5 during a temporary vacancy in the premiership in 1924 offered a peerage to Asquith, a former Prime Minister who had just lost his seat in a general election.

Otherwise the Queen's official acts are done on the advice of her Ministers, notably the Prime Minister. 'Advice' here is a polite word for instruction after consultation. An important exception, discussed later in this chapter, is the choice of Prime Minister in certain unusual situations. Even here account must be taken of constitutional principles and precedents, though there is some discretion as to the persons whose advice may be sought. A criticism one could make is that the forms and costumes of our public ceremonies might well be simplified in this latter part of the twentieth century.

THE ROYAL PREROGATIVE

Our traditional unwritten Constitution vests the legal powers and responsibilities of government in 'the Crown', a convenient expression to cover the Queen acting through or on the advice of her Ministers–'her' Ministers, not ours. The summoning and dissolution of Parliament, the conduct of foreign affairs and negotiation of treaties, the making of war and peace, the defence of the realm, the maintenance of order, the making of judicial and other official appointments, the administration of dependent territories, the responsibility for handling national finance, the control of the civil and defence services, all these are matters of royal prerogative. When Parliament grants additional powers relating to such matters as transport, education, social welfare, control of prices and wages, police and prisons, housing, agriculture or aviation, the statutory powers are usually conferred directly on the Minister concerned, but he is still a Minister of the Crown. Most Bills are introduced by Ministers in connection with the affairs of their departments; and although they do so in the same way as unofficial members of Parliament, this means in effect that most legislation is initiated by the Government. Thus the Government has been called the starting-point and mainspring of action. The converse idea–derived from the French Revolution – that political power is delegated by the individual voter to the Legislature, and thence to an Executive dependent on the Legislature, does not fit in with our institutions and leads to different consequences. Instead of a choice between the existing Government and the Opposition as the prospective Government, with periods of strong, stable administration as the norm, it would involve proportional representation among

23

numerous parties, leading usually to unstable administration and perhaps eventually to one-party government.

CONSTITUTIONAL CONVENTIONS

The transformation from legal theory to political fact in our system of government has been largely made by constitutional conventions, such as that requiring the Queen to give her assent to Bills passed by both Houses of Parliament. Although conventions have the advantage of flexibility, reliance on them has the drawback of vagueness and uncertainty. Opinions may differ not only concerning the scope of a given convention, but about whether a supposed convention exists at all. Is it a convention that the Queen may no longer dismiss a Government, as distinct from individual Ministers on the Prime Minister's advice? A Ministry has not been dismissed in this country since 1783, but this fact does not of itself establish a convention. Suppose a Government which retains a majority in the Commons has in the Queen's opinion clearly lost the support of the majority of the electorate and pursues an 'unconstitutional' course of conduct, such as introducing Bills for prolonging the life of Parliament, gerrymandering of constituencies or major modifications of the electoral system in the interests of its own party. Sir Ivor Jennings thought that in such exceptional circumstances the Queen would be justified in dismissing her Ministers, provided an alternative Government was willing to take office. Even the question of how the Head of State is to know whether a Prime Minister has lost the confidence of the elected Chamber has been the subject of controversy in Nigeria and Malaysia. Is a letter signed by a majority of members sufficient, or must a vote be taken in the House? And the question whether the Queen may refuse the Prime Minister's request for a dissolution is discussed later in this and in the next chapter.

Generally the power of the Sovereign in modern times is limited, in Bagehot's words, to the right to be consulted, the right to encourage and the right to warn; but the influence of a monarch who has been on the throne for some years may increase. Few

24

Ministers, if any, will have had such wide and continuous experience. This influence can best be exercised by mediating between party leaders in times of crisis, in bringing the protagonists together and suggesting a solution but without pressing it. Examples could be given from the reign of George 5 in connection with the Parliament Bill 1910–11, Irish Home Rule in 1914, the economic crisis in 1931 and the negotiations for the Anglo-Irish treaty. A hereditary monarchy here is in a more favourable position than a Governor-General who is appointed for five years and may have been a politician. The Queen's Private Secretary, a post that has now been established for the last hundred years, should not be overlooked. The Private Secretary, who is sworn of the Privy Council, seeks advice informally from various sources—members of the Government, members of the Opposition and other public officers—and then briefs the Queen.

THE GOVERNMENT AND MINISTERIAL RESPONSIBILITY

The Government, or Ministry as it used to be called, consists nowadays of the holders of nearly one hundred political offices, most of them sitting in the House of Commons. This means that nearly a hundred members of Parliament, or perhaps a third of the Government's supporters in the House, have a vested interest in voting for the Government. The older offices, such as those of Lord Chancellor, First Lord of the Treasury, Chancellor of the Exchequer, Lord President of the Council and Secretary of State have a common law origin. New offices can be created by prerogative, but as an Act of Parliament is necessary to authorise salaries, offices in modern times are created by statute. Functions may be re-allocated among existing departments by statutory Orders in Council. Thus the Minister for the Civil Service recently got certain functions of the Treasury concerning the organisation, conduct and pay of the civil service. In initiating the Bills or Orders for creating and abolishing departments, or changing their names and functions, the Prime Minister has a pretty free hand. A rationalisation of the classification of government departments was suggested by the Machinery of Government

Committee in 1918, and this is a favourite exercise among political scientists. But every Prime Minister has his own views on this matter, and makes changes to suit the Government's policy and his design for personal appointments. It would be difficult to discern any coherent pattern in the frequent changes made in departmental organisation and nomenclature during the last fifty years. Some changes, such as those affecting the Colonial Office, Dominions Office, Commonwealth Relations and Commonwealth Affairs, explain themselves in the light of external events. Some, like the setting up of the short-lived Department of Economic Affairs in 1964, are inexplicable except on the ground of personalities or Mr. Wilson's theory of tension between departments. Others reflect shifting emphases or propaganda in rival party policies, for example, the change of title in 1951 from Local Government and Planning to Housing and Local Government.

All Ministers are required by convention to be members of one or other House of Parliament. The number who may sit in the Commons is limited by statute. Mr. Wilson, when he became Prime Minister, wanted to increase the number of Ministers and also to give experience of office to a large number of colleagues. He was surprised to find that the House of Commons Disqualification Act 1957 limited the number who might sit in the Commons to 70. Pending the passing of a new Act raising the number to 91, he appointed to 14 offices not in the schedule to the Act 1957, and to 12 offices without remuneration, conduct which was contrary to the spirit of the statute. If the Prime Minister wishes to appoint to a Minsterial post someone from outside Parliament, that person must either be given a peerage (nowadays it would be a life peerage) or else he must get himself elected at a by-election. This can usually be assured by giving a peerage to a Government supporter with a safe seat, so as to create a vacancy. So when in 1964 Mr. Cousins, a trade union official, and Mr. Gordon Walker, who had been defeated at Smethwick at the recent general election, were appointed to Cabinet posts Mr. Cousins was duly elected to Parliament but Mr. Walker was defeated at a by-election and resigned office next day. Some Commonwealth Constitutions require a Minister who is not in the legislature to be elected within a time limit of (say) three months or else resign, but our convention sets no limit, except a reasonable time.

The individual responsibility of Ministers is owed by law to the Crown and by convention to Parliament. The sanction for political misdemeanours as distinct from criminal offences was formerly impeachment, which fell into disuse early in the nineteenth century. A Minister's conventional responsibility means, not necessarily or usually moral culpability, but accountability to the Commons, the obligation to explain and answer questions concerning the affairs of his department. Following the report of the Crichel Down Enquiry in 1954 it was stated in the House that a Minister must accept responsibility for the actions of the civil servants in his department, and he is expected to defend them from public criticism since they cannot answer back, unless they have done something reprehensible that he forbad, or of which he disapproves and of which he did not have and could not reasonably be expected to have had previous knowledge. In the latter case, which is unusual, he may dismiss them. In some Commonwealth countries Ministerial responsibility for the acts of civil servants is said to be less strict, though the degree of responsibility in this country is often exaggerated. The criticism found in the Fulton Report and elsewhere against the secrecy and anonymity of the civil service, on the other hand, ignores the doctrine of Ministerial responsibility. Not only is it the duty of civil servants to shield their Minister from public blame, but if their anonymity were broken down and they dealt with the public in their own names, they would lose the protection of their Minister. The thinking behind such suggestions may be due to the drawing of a false analogy with systems where the doctrine of Ministerial responsibility either does not exist or is not fully developed.

It has been argued that resignation is no longer an effective sanction for individual Ministerial responsibility because it can be obviated by a reshuffle of posts or by the protective solidarity of colleagues, and anyway a Minister who resigns can be appointed soon afterwards to another post. Resignations are admittedly not common, but one could mention the cases of Austen Chamberlain in 1917, Montagu in 1922, Thomas in 1936, Dalton in 1947, Dugdale in 1954 (though he was not strictly responsible) and Profumo in 1963.

Ministerial responsibility is also by convention collective. The collective responsibility is owed both to the Sovereign, to whom Ministers must give unanimous advice, and to Parliament and the nation to which they must show a united front however much they disagree behind the scenes. If a Minister cannot agree with his colleagues on a question of policy, he should either keep quiet about it or resign: if his department is directly involved, resignation is the only course. Thus Mr. Eden, Duff Cooper and Lord Cranborne resigned over the policy of appeasing the dictators at the time of Munich in 1938, Aneurin Bevan resigned in 1951 over cuts in the health service, and Mr. Thorneycroft in 1957 over increases in the estimates. Lord Longford resigned quietly from Mr. Wilson's Government, and Mr. Cousins and Mr. Brown more noisily. After Mr. Callaghan had voted against Mrs. Castle's proposals for trade union reforms at a meeting of the Labour party national executive committee in the spring of 1969, Mr. Wilson is said to have reminded his Cabinet colleagues of the principle of collective responsibility, of their duty not to oppose Cabinet policy.

The collective responsibility of Ministers not in the Cabinet is passive rather than active, since they are not usually consulted on matters that do not concern their departments. Sir Edward Boyle did resign from a junior post in Sir Anthony Eden's Government in 1956 over Suez, but he was given another junior post next year by Mr. Macmillan, who had confirmed his Government's support for the Suez policy. The Eden Cabinet was widely thought to have been divided over Suez, though this was not admitted. Mr. Wilson's Labour Cabinet were divided over devaluation, the Common Market, legal sanctions against trade unions, and increased national health charges for teeth and spectacles.

THE GOVERNMENT

CONSTITUTIONAL POSITION OF CIVIL SERVANTS

There is a long tradition of the official impartiality of civil servants in this country. A civil servant must resign his post before standing as a candidate for a Parliamentary election. With regard to other political activities, Government regulations have to effect a compromise between two conflicting principles: one, the desirability that all citizens should have a voice in public affairs and that as many as possible should be able to play an active part in public life; the other, the public interest that the impartiality of the civil service should be maintained. Civil service regulations therefore distinguish between three classes of civil servants and between national and local politics. Unlike those in the federal capital of Washington, none of them are disfranchised. The senior grades who are most likely to come into contact with the public are restricted from taking an active part in national, though not in local, politics. The remaining executive and clerical officers may take part in national as well as local politics, subject to a code of 'discretion' with regard to the expression of views on governmental policy and national political issues. Manipulative and industrial workers may engage in both national and local politics, except when on duty or on official premises or while wearing uniform.

The precise legal position of civil servants, on the other hand, is in need of clarification. They are servants of the Crown, appointed and (in theory) dismissible at pleasure by the Crown. Although in practice civil servants have considerable security of tenure and are protected by influential trade unions, judicial decisions are uncertain and conflicting as to whether a civil servant has any (and, if so what) remedy if he is dismissed contrary to the terms of his engagement, or whether if his engagement is properly terminated he can recover arrears of salary earned by him. In *Sutton* v. *Attorney-General* (1923) the House of Lords assumed that a contractual relationship subsists between the Crown and a civil servant, the terms of which are enforceable by the latter; but the attention of their Lordships was not drawn to this question and it was not argued. There are *dicta* in other cases to the effect that

29

there is no contract of service such as can be enforced against the Crown, even to the extent of claiming arrears of salary due. Mr. Justice Diplock expressed the opposite opinion *obiter* in *Riordan* v. *War Office* (1959), but Mr. Justice Gorman avoided deciding the question in two cases arising out of the Government's 'pay pause' in January 1964.

THE CABINET AND ITS DEVELOPMENT

The Cabinet, which came to be the chief organ of government by the nineteenth century and was still generally so regarded down to recent years, is a product of constitutional conventions. Its members hold various legal offices by virtue of which they exercise common law and statutory powers and receive statutory salaries, but the Cabinet as a body had no legal existence until it was recognised by an Act of Parliament in 1937 dealing with salaries. This Act is now replaced by the Ministerial Salaries Consolidation Act 1965 which, after prescribing salaries for the holders of the Ministerial offices specified in a schedule, goes on to say that the salary of the Lord President of the Council or the Chancellor of the Duchy of Lancaster 'when not a member of the Cabinet' shall be determined (within the permitted maximum) by the First Lord of the Treasury, and that the date on which the holder of one of these offices 'becomes or ceases to be a Member of the Cabinet' shall be published in the London Gazette, and any such notification shall be conclusive evidence for that purpose. So the Prime Minister (as First Lord of the Treasury) decides whether the principal officer of the Privy Council or the Duchy of Lancaster shall be a member of the Cabinet and whether to notify the London Gazette, and then decides how much less than the statutory maximum that Minister shall be paid.

The practice of withdrawing the discussion and direction of policy from the Privy Council into the hands of a few of the King's *confidential* advisers developed during the seventeenth and eighteenth centuries; but owing to the confusing terminology of contemporary writers, the secrecy of the proceedings, the lack of official and connected records, and the fact that during most of this period the practice was unpopular both with Parliament and in the country and therefore was not openly avowed, the history is obscure. Parliament objected to the secrecy of the deliberations, because it made it difficult to identify who were the Ministers responsible. Two clauses in the Act of Settlement 1700 which never came into effect sought to put a stop to the practice, by providing not only (as we have seen) that no person holding a place of profit under the Crown might sit in the House of Commons, but also that matters hitherto discussed in the Privy Council should be dealt with there and not elsewhere, and all resolutions should be signed by the Ministers present. The better opinion seems to be that the Cabinet, although it grew out of the Privy Council, cannot at any stage of its history be identified with any particular committee of the Council. Its development was helped by the gradual abstention of George 1 and 2 from meetings. The idea that the Cabinet should all be members of the same party was of gradual growth, as was the development of the political parties themselves. The conventions now operative need hardly be looked for before the Reform Act 1832, or even before the Representation of the People Act 1867. During Victoria's long reign the Sovereign ceased to enjoy a personal choice of Ministers, although that Queen could still successfully object to the appointment of particular individuals to all but the highest office.

FUNCTIONS OF THE CABINET

The Haldane Committee on the Machinery of Government in 1918 summarised the main functions of the Cabinet at that time as being: '(a) the final determination of the policy to be submitted to Parliament; (b) the supreme control of the national executive in accordance with the policy prescribed by Parliament; and (c) the continuous co-ordination and delimitation of the several Departments of State'. The expression 'final determination of policy' if applied to the present day would disguise the extent of the Prime Minister's influence in the Cabinet; and 'in accordance with the policy prescribed by Parliament' obscures the fact that, because of the Government's tight control of its party in the

Commons, Parliament prescribes what the Government wants. Between the wars emphasis was placed on the co-ordinating function of the Cabinet between the Executive and the Legislature and among the organs of the Executive themselves. After the last war L. S. Amery described the Cabinet as the directing instrument of government. 'It is the Cabinet', he said, 'which controls Parliament and governs the country.'

Whether we still have Cabinet government is a question we shall leave until we have discussed the position of the Prime Minister. Until recently, at least, most important matters of policy were discussed by the Cabinet, except membership of the Cabinet itself, appointments and honours, and the exercise by the Home Secretary of the prerogative of mercy (which has lost most of its importance since the abolition of the death penalty for murder). For reasons of secrecy, however, the Budget proposals are disclosed orally a few days only before the Chancellor of the Exchequer is to introduce them into the Commons, and for diplomatic reasons it is not always practicable to consult the Cabinet before taking action in foreign affairs. Every attempt is made to promote unanimity, a Prime Minister preferring to collect the sense of the meeting and only rarely taking a vote.

COMPOSITION AND SIZE OF THE CABINET

In selecting his Cabinet the Prime Minister has to consider a number of factors. First there is the influence of members in the party and the country; some are defeated or aspiring rivals for the leadership. There is the authority of members in the House and their skill in debate. Then it may be expedient to include one or two who represent party views to the left or right of the Prime Minister. Scotland and Wales must be represented. The Cabinet needs spokesmen in the House of Lords in addition to the Lord Chancellor. A colleague little known to the public may be chosen because, without having qualities of popular appeal, he is valued for his wise counsel. One thing not considered requisite is that a Minister, whether in the Cabinet or not, should be an expert in the affairs of his department: expertise can be left to the civil servants who work for him. Allocation of Ministers to the various departments depends on the importance both of the office and of the man. The Prime Minister can reshuffle his colleagues throughout his period of office. All Ministerial offices are regarded by convention as being continuously at the Prime Minister's disposal. He has no need to advise the Queen to dismiss a Minister: he can simply call for the colleague's resignation, perhaps after a polite exchange of letters.

All Cabinet Ministers are made members of the Privy Council, if they are not so already. This tradition binds them to the Privy Councillor's oath in addition to the Official Secrets Acts.

Most recent discussions about the Cabinet have been on the questions of size and composition in relation to efficiency. The modern Cabinet is larger than Elizabeth I's Privy Council. Between the wars membership tended to exceed twenty. After the last war the number was reduced to below twenty for a time, but Sir Alec Douglas-Home and Mr. Wilson both had Cabinets of twenty-three, the latter being reduced to twenty-one. A large Cabinet is said to favour the power of the Prime Minister, though it is not suggested that this is the motive behind the increase. The problem for the Prime Minister must be whom to leave out. First there are the departments that must always be represented—the Exchequer, Foreign Affairs, the Lord Chancellor, the Home Secretary, Scotland, Wales and so on. Secondly there are departments which are considered specially important for current policy, such as education, housing or local government. Then the Prime Minister may wish to create or upgrade special departments for some new experiment or in order to neutralise the influence of dangerous rivals. After all this, however much he may have hoped when he took office to keep the number down, the Prime Minister finds that there are several promising young colleagues who in the long-term interests of the party need experience of high office. So with the general expansion of government work Cabinets grow.

L. S. Amery, who had considerable experience as a Cabinet Minister between the wars, expressed the opinion in his *Thoughts on the Constitution* that 'a Cabinet consisting of a score of overworked departmental Ministers is quite incapable of either thinking out a definite policy, or of securing its effective and consistent execution'. The one thing that is hardly ever discussed, he continued, is general policy, with the result that there is very little Cabinet policy as such on any subject. Amery suggested a Cabinet of about half-a-dozen, all free from departmental duties, not only to deal with current administrative questions, but also to have regular meetings set aside for the discussion of future policy. Standing Committees to co-ordinate the work of groups of departments with overlapping interests and presided over by members of the Cabinet free from routine work, would expedite the administrative work of the Cabinet, but there should also be a group of standing committees–corresponding to the Defence Committee–for the study of policy in such fields as external affairs, economics and social welfare, each with an adequate research and planning staff. The Prime Minister would be chairman of each of these policy committees, one of his colleagues being deputy chairman. The latter would be not only a co-ordinator but a Policy Minister for a group of departments. On important issues affecting national security or less directly concerned with party politics, leaders of the Opposition could properly be brought into discussions of these standing committees.

Another very experienced Cabinet Minister, Lord Samuel, thought that the ideal number for a Cabinet was ten. A recent leading article in *The Times* suggests that the ideal number would be fifteen. Churchill's experiment in 1951–53 of assigning several Ministers, popularly known as Overlords, to supervise groups of other Ministers and publishing their names and sphere of authority, although it had some administrative success, was politically a failure. Objections were raised that the practice degraded the Ministers who were supervised, and that it confused the responsibility to Parliament. One way of reducing the Cabinet would be by further merger of departments on the lines of Defence (including the three Service Departments), and Foreign and Commonwealth Affairs. Mr. Wilson in October 1969 liquidated the ill-starred Department of Economic Affairs, gave Health and Social

Security to the Secretary of State for Social Services, put Housing and Transport under a Secretary of State for Local Government and Regional Planning, and handed over Power to the Minister of Technology. It has been suggested that a Department of Economics could include the Treasury, Economic Affairs, Technology, Trade and Labour; a Ministry of Justice could take over the relevant functions of the Lord Chancellor and the Home Secretary, and a Secretary of State for England the remaining functions of the Home Office and Local Government.

Small War Cabinets were formed in the two world wars, varying from five members (all but one without departmental duties) to nine (mostly with departmental duties). Outside experts, as well as non-Cabinet Ministers, were summoned to advise or report. In the first war General Smuts sat with the War Cabinet although he was not a member of either House, and several meetings were held with Dominion Prime Ministers in what was called the 'Imperial War Cabinet'. In the last war the Cabinet at one time included Mr. Casey, an Australian who was not a member of Parliament but held the post of Minister of State resident in the Middle East, and Lord Halifax continued to be available after becoming Ambassador to the United States. In both wars the Dominions were invited to send representatives from time to time.

Ministers who are not members of the Cabinet may be called in if matters specially affecting their departments are under discussion. The Chiefs of Staff may be present when defence questions are being discussed, and the permanent heads of the Treasury or the Foreign Office may be summoned. Otherwise civil servants, apart from the Secretary to the Cabinet, are rarely present except in the Legislation Committee.

Some people think that outside experts–economists and so on– should be included in the Cabinet; but however useful they may be as temporary civil servants, it would offend the principle of responsible government if they were not members of Parliament.

There is a recent tendency for an 'inner' Cabinet to be formed, composed not of Ministers without departmental duties but of those heads of the most important departments whom the Prime

Minister finds congenial as colleagues. According to the press Mr. Callaghan, Home Secretary and a past contender for the Labour leadership, was recently excluded from the inner Cabinet because he was in disagreement with the Prime Minister on matters of policy. This is an interesting development, as it echoes a division between the outer and inner Cabinet that took place in the reign of George 2, and it was from the inner body that the modern Cabinet grew. On the other hand, differences on policy expressed at the Cabinet table would not be enough to exclude a Minister from the Cabinet altogether.

Another twentieth-century development is the practice of setting up Cabinet committees, whether standing or *ad hoc*, for special services or particular problems. This also is an echo of earlier history, for the Cabinet itself originated as some kind of committee of the Privy Council. Because of the principle of the unity and collective responsibility of the Cabinet, it is not usual to disclose the existence of a Cabinet committee, its terms of reference or the name of its chairman during the lifetime of a Government. Since the war standing committees have included the Defence Committee – about which, paradoxically, we are told most in White Papers – the Home Affairs Committee, the Legislation Committee, the Public Expenditure Survey Committee and Committees on Economic Policy and Social Services. The new Parliamentary Committee covers the whole range of Government work, including long-term questions.

Experience shows that it is difficult to separate policy from administration except under pressure of war or other emergency, and the general conclusion seems to be that it is not desirable to try to do so. A Minister who is himself involved in administration has a better understanding when it comes to the formation of policy. Each Prime Minister must deal empirically with the question. It is not a matter for which one can legislate, either literally, or metaphorically.

THE GOVERNMENT

THE PRIME MINISTER: DEVELOPMENT AND FUNCTIONS OF THE OFFICE

The primary function of the Prime Minister is to form a Government and to preside over the Cabinet. The position, which may be said to have begun with Walpole and the younger Pitt, was brought about by convention. One Minister came to have the special confidence of the King, combined with a pre-eminence among the other Ministers and ability to get and keep a majority in the Commons. This was a time when party allegiances were less settled than now, and he was assisted by the patronage at his disposal as First Lord of the Treasury, from which office he derived his salary. Following the extensions of the franchise and the development of political parties during the nineteenth century, the position of Prime Minister was firmly established by the personalities of Disraeli and Gladstone. Apart from the Treaty of Berlin 1878, the post is not mentioned in a legal document before the present century. It is now recognised in a few documents, notably the Ministerial Salaries Consolidation Act 1965 (replacing the Ministers of the Crown Act 1937) which provides a salary for the 'Prime Minister and First Lord of the Treasury', and a pension for any person who has been Prime Minister and First Lord of the Treasury. It is therefore unlikely that these two posts will be held separately in future, though the Act does not require them to be held together, nor does it prevent them from being held jointly with another office, such as Minister of Defence, subject to the general rule that only one salary is payable.

It is the Prime Minister who nominates the other Ministers, chooses from among them the Cabinet, reshuffles their posts and calls for their individual resignations. He is the main channel of communication between the Cabinet and the Sovereign, although other Ministers – for example, the Foreign Secretary, the Chancellor of the Exchequer and the Home Secretary – may communicate with the Sovereign on matters concerning their special responsibilities. He gives advice to his colleagues on matters before they come before the Cabinet. He is the leader of his party, either having been chosen Prime Minister because he was the leader of the largest party in the Commons, or having been elected leader because he became Prime Minister. Churchill, never what is called a good party man, when appointed Prime Minister in 1940 tried at first to get on without taking over the leadership of the Conservative party, but he soon found this impracticable. Although some other Minister is usually called Leader of the House, the Prime Minister is primarily responsible for planning the business of the House, in which he has a residuary obligation to speak in debates and to answer questions on matters of general policy. The Prime Minister sees that Cabinet decisions are carried out by the departments, and is in specially close touch with the Foreign Office. He communicates with heads of government in other Commonwealth countries, and presides when they meet in this country. He nominates to a number of important Crown appointments, including the Lords of Appeal in Ordinary, the Lords Justices of Appeal, Bishops and Deans of the Church of England, peers, Privy Councillors, Regius Professors and most honours. As First Lord of the Treasury he approves the senior appointments in the civil service, though this is largely formal.

CHOICE OF PRIME MINISTER

The ordinary case is where a Government has been defeated at a general election: the convention is that the Prime Minister resigns, and with him the other Ministers, and the Sovereign on the advice of the resigning Prime Minister sends for the Leader of the Opposition in the Commons. The latter somewhat paradoxically has received a statutory salary since 1937 (unless he is in receipt of an ex-Prime Minister's pension); and the Ministerial Salaries Consolidation Act 1965 defines him for salary purposes as that member of the House who is for the time being Leader in the House of the party in opposition to Her Majesty's Government having the greatest numerical strength in the House. Both main parties out of office elect a leader and so there should seldom be doubt. In this way Mr. Harold Wilson became Prime Minister in 1964. The position would be similar if the Government were

38

defeated on a vote regarded as one of confidence in the House of Commons in such circumstances that a dissolution was not appropriate (for example, because one or more general elections have already recently been held); but owing to the strength of party allegiance the defeat of a majority Government in the Commons has become rare in modern times. Nor has the Sovereign any real discretion where a Prime Minister with an absolute majority retires on personal, as distinct from political, grounds, such as ill-health or old age, leaving an obvious second-in-command. Although it is probably not proper for a *retiring* Prime Minister to proffer advice as to his successor, he can make his views known beforehand, and anyway the Sovereign is free to consult him as well as his colleagues. In this way Sir Anthony Eden succeeded Churchill in 1955.

In exceptional cases the Sovereign is still called upon to exercise a limited personal discretion. There may be no one party with an absolute majority in the House of Commons and it may be a question of forming or breaking up a coalition. The Sovereign may then consult all interested parties with a view to forming a Government that can command a majority in the House. So in 1931, when the economic crisis led to the disintegration of Ramsay MacDonald's minority Labour Government, George 5 took the initiative in the formation of a coalition called the 'National Government'. The King consulted the Conservative and Liberal leaders, both of whom had a considerable following in the House, and then asked MacDonald to resume office as head of a predominantly Conservative coalition in spite of the defection of most of his own party. This Government lasted until after the King's silver jubilee in 1935. Again, in 1940 a successor had to be found when Neville Chamberlain, the Conservative Prime Minister, resigned because he felt he had lost the confidence of his own party in the conduct of the war; also he wanted a coalition to be formed, and Labour had let it be known that they would not serve under him whereas they would serve under Churchill. In an informal discussion with Chamberlain, the King suggested Lord Halifax, whom Chamberlain himself would have preferred;

but Chamberlain recounted an earlier conference between Halifax, Churchill and himself, in which Halifax expressed the view that it would be impracticable to try to lead the Government from the Lords, especially in time of war, as he would have the responsibility without the power. The King then asked Chamberlain his advice, and accordingly sent for Churchill.

The other exceptional case is when a Prime Minister dies in office or resigns on personal grounds of ill-health or old age leaving no obvious successor. It has not been the practice of the Parliamentary Conservative party in the past to elect a deputy leader; nor does the Parliamentary Labour party do so when in office. So George 5 made the celebrated choice of Baldwin rather than Lord Curzon in 1923, and Her Majesty chose Mr. Macmillan rather than Mr. Butler in 1957 and the Earl of Home rather than various rivals in 1963. On the latter occasion Lord Home did not accept at once, but waited until he had assured himself that he was able to form a Government.

The question whether there is now a convention that a peer should not be appointed Prime Minister has become largely academic since the Peerage Act 1953 allowed hereditary peerages to be disclaimed, though as there is a time limit for disclaimer the question could possibly arise. In Churchill's coalition Government during the last war, Attlee (leader of the Labour party) was called Deputy Prime Minister; but when in 1942 George 5 asked Churchill to advise him as to his successor if the Prime Minister should die as a result of enemy action abroad, he advised the King to send for Mr. Eden; and before the Yalta Conference in 1945 Churchill, at the King's request, advised that Sir John Anderson should be his successor if both he and Mr. Eden were killed on their forthcoming journey. More than once since the war a Minister has been called Deputy Prime Minister, but George 6 expressed his objection as it would imply a line of succession and so restrict the royal prerogative. We have probably now reached the stage when those concerned would prefer the Sovereign whenever possible to be relieved of the invidious task of making a choice. It appears that in New Zealand, and probably Australia, if a Prime Minister died in office the Governor-General would wait a few days until his party had elected a new leader, unless they had already elected a Deputy. A similar convention could well be established in this country.

CABINET SECRETARIAT

Cabinet minutes were not kept during Victoria's reign. The Prime Minister sat down and wrote a weekly letter to the Queen in his own handwriting. The other Ministers were expected to remember what had been decided and to act upon it. Lloyd George formed a Cabinet Office in 1916 out of the secretariat of the Committee of Imperial Defence. His reason for doing this, perhaps as a temporary expedient, was pressure of work; but by doing so he institutionalised the great powers he had assumed, and so enabled them to be transmitted to successors who had not his personality and drive. As the Cabinet was a body unknown to the law, staff salaries continued to be paid out of the Treasury vote.

The Haldane Committee in 1918 recommended that the Cabinet Office should be retained for the purpose of collecting and arranging the agenda, of providing the information and material necessary for the Cabinet's deliberations, and of drawing up the results for communication to the departments concerned. The advantage of minutes is that they enable the Cabinet conclusions, and the reasons on which they are based, to be circulated to its members, who might otherwise go away with different recollections or none as to what was decided and why. The Secretary of the Cabinet holds the key position in the public service. Bridges and Normanbrook doubled the part of (Joint) Permanent Secretary to the Treasury, and the latter was made a Privy Councillor. More recently the Secretary has been separated from the Treasury. The Secretariat also serves Cabinet committees. In theory it is responsible to the Cabinet as a body, but as it is in continuous touch with the Prime Minister as chairman it sometimes looks as if it takes its orders from him. The Secretary may be regarded as the Prime Minister's chief official adviser. It has been suggested that the Cabinet Office should be turned into something more like the President's White House Office, with its counsellors and special assistants–a powerhouse generating ideas, providing the President with information on all aspects of public life. An exact copy would obviously run foul of Cabinet responsibility; but special assistants could be provided for the Cabinet and its committees and also for Ministers. It is not clear how this proposal differs in effect from an expansion of the practice already adopted in varying degrees by Churchill and Mr. Wilson of bringing in outsiders as temporary civil servants, except that this does not involve the questionable modification of the Official Secrets Acts advocated by those who put forward the other plan.

PRIME MINISTER'S POSITION IN RELATION TO THE CABINET

The Prime Minister's pre-eminence is due largely to his standing as a leader in the eyes of the public. Although electors are said to vote mainly for a party image, a modern general election is in one sense the election of a Prime Minister who embodies that image. The Prime Minister's hold over his colleagues owes much to the fact that Ministerial posts are in his gift, though he has more freedom in reshuffling them than in making the original appointments. In the 'massacre' of 1962 Mr. Macmillan without warning called for the resignation of no fewer than seven members of the Cabinet, including his old friend Lord Kilmuir. The Prime Minister can determine the scope of the various offices, as well as taking over additional office himself or assuming control of foreign or Commonwealth affairs. Mr. Wilson, for example, set up a Department of Economic Affairs to balance the power of the Treasury, and then later assumed control of economic affairs. A colleague's career, it is said, could be ruined by his appointment to a hopeless assignment.

The Prime Minister knows more than any of his colleagues what is going on. He largely controls the Cabinet agenda by initiating most items. He may, like any artful chairman, try to avoid discussion on a particular item, though he cannot prevent a matter from being put on the agenda if a colleague presses for it. Baldwin once closed a Cabinet meeting by leaving the room when Neville Chamberlain wanted to discuss House of Lords reform, but it seems that this matter was not on the agenda; if it had been on the agenda Baldwin could hardly have prevented its discussion. If Churchill had done such a thing it would be more likely because he wanted to go to the races. Attlee's decision to develop atomic weapons did not go further than the Defence Committee, though the minutes were circulated to members of the Cabinet who could have taken up the matter if they had wished. Sir Anthony Eden excluded discussion about entry into the Common Market, and only informed the Cabinet of the plan for the Suez operation four days before Israel attacked Egypt, but he had the support of his chief colleagues. The Prime Minister also has the advantage of prior reports and informal discussions on items that are going to be put on the agenda. He it is who sums up the sense of the meeting: other Ministers do not ask for a vote to be taken. On the other hand he could hardly sum up *against* the sense of the meeting.

It is very difficult for a Prime Minister with a majority to be overthrown. This can only be done by a Cabinet *coup* (but often there is neither unanimity among senior Ministers nor agreement over a successor), or else by a meeting of backbenchers, in which case the result may be a general election, the shortening of the Government's term of office and many seats lost. In the case of Asquith in 1916 there was need of a wartime coalition, and in the case of Lloyd George in 1922 the end of a coalition was wanted. Neville Chamberlain in 1940 did not let matters go as far as this before resigning. Yet a Prime Minister cannot bulldoze his Cabinet. Even Churchill gave way on occasions when the majority were against him.

In the end the position of the Prime Minister in relation to his Cabinet is variable and depends on the nature and strength of their personalities, not only that of the Prime Minister but also those of his colleagues. Lloyd George had abler colleagues than Neville Chamberlain, as Atlee had abler colleagues than Mr. Wilson. Lloyd George and Chamberlain were the most autocratic Prime

Ministers in the present century, and ultimately they were both rejected. Churchill was a constitutionalist and on occasion compromised or bowed to defeat.

PRIME MINISTER AND THE TIMING OF DISSOLUTION

In considering the relation of the Prime Minister to his colleagues, the crucial question is that of deciding on a dissolution of Parliament. Asquith wrote in his memoirs that this question was always submitted to the Cabinet for ultimate decision; but in 1918 Lloyd George and Bonar Law, as the party leaders in the Coalition Government, alone decided on the dissolution. The lapse of time since the last general election in 1910 had apparently caused Ministers to forget that this was an innovation. Baldwin did not consult the Cabinet formally in 1923 or 1935, nor did Churchill do so in 1945. It is now current practice–some even call it a convention–that the decision when to 'advise' a dissolution, so vital in the national interest, is taken–not by the Cabinet–but by the Prime Minister after consulting a few intimate colleagues, the Chief Whip and the Chairman of the party. The Cabinet might have revived their collective power in 1923, but did not attempt to do so. An exceptional case was 1924, when Ramsay MacDonald was head of a minority Government. Then the Cabinet decided on a general election because they had already agreed to regard as votes of censure the forthcoming Opposition motions concerning the withdrawal of the prosecution against Campbell, the editor of the *Workers' Weekly*.

It is important that we should revert to the former practice of Cabinet decision, but not easy to see quite how this can be ensured. A change of attitude on the part of Cabinet Ministers is required, or else a reversion on the part of the Queen to the nineteenth-century practice of granting a dissolution to the Cabinet rather than to an individual. On the rare occasion of a premature dissolution in New Zealand, the Prime Minister is expected to indicate to the Governor-General that he has the support of the Cabinet.

The importance of the question lies in its effect on Parliamentary

44

elections, discussed in the next chapter, and not in its effect on the Prime Minister's party. An attempt to browbeat back-benchers with the threat of dissolution would now be largely bluff, and would no longer be effective if the party were divided and its morale in the country low. Members fear losing the party Whip and consequent re-nomination, rather than a general election that would probably bring down the Government and the Prime Minister himself with it. Hence the warning Mr. Wilson gave to recalcitrant members in 1967 that they might not get their dog licences renewed when they fell due.

There is no precedent in this century of a Prime Minister, whose party has a majority in the Commons, asking for a dissolution in order to strengthen his weakening hold over his own party. If he did ask for a dissolution in such circumstances the better opinion is that the Queen would be entitled, perhaps would have a duty, to refuse. In the normal case when the Sovereign grants a dissolution this is on the assumption that the Prime Minister is acting as leader on behalf of his party. Otherwise the electorate could not be expected to decide the question of leadership. So if the Sovereign could find another Prime Minister who was able to carry on the government for a reasonable period, she would be justified in refusing a dissolution. Something like this happened in South Africa in 1939 when the question was whether South Africa should enter the war: the Governor-General refused a dissolution to Hertzog, who resigned and was replaced by Smuts who succeeded in forming a Government.

'CABINET GOVERNMENT', 'PRIME MINISTERIAL GOVERNMENT' OR 'PRESIDENTIAL GOVERNMENT'?

There is a general view that the Prime Minister's power has increased considerably in modern times, but a difference of opinion as to how far he has outstripped his colleagues and how long the process has taken. Some writers say that we no longer have 'Cabinet Government' as we used to know it, but 'Prime Ministerial Government', a change that has taken place according to some since the last war and according to others since before that. Policy is not usually initiated by the Cabinet. Decisions tend to be taken either by the Prime Minister alone or by him after consulting one or two Ministers, or else by Cabinet committees or *ad hoc* meetings of the departmental Ministers concerned. To these factors is added the unification and centralisation of the expanding civil service under the Prime Minister, formerly through the Treasury and now through the Civil Service Ministry. On the other hand the Cabinet remains the channel for settling and co-ordinating priorities. As J. P. Mackintosh says, it 'reconciles, records and authorises'. Mr. Crossman in his introduction to the Fontana edition of Bagehot's *English Constitution* published in 1963, before he took office in Mr. Wilson's Government, stated categorically that since the last war we have seen 'the final transformation of Cabinet Government into Prime Ministerial Government'.

Mr. Wilson, speaking tactfully and more temperately while in office, insists (as reported in *The Listener*, February 9, 1967) that the Cabinet is supreme. All matters of great national importance or which might raise important political undertones, he says, ought to be put before the Cabinet; although the Prime Minister must see that through delegation to committees the Cabinet is not overloaded with business. He sees the role of the Prime Minister as 'if not that of a managing director, as that of an executive chairman'. According to Mr. Wilson, power still lies in the Cabinet, but as the Cabinet must keep the confidence of the House, it is the Cabinet in Parliament. The power-base lies in 'his party in Parliament'.

Another view is that the process of increase in the Prime Minister's power has been gradual and uneven over quite a long period, and that his present power is liable to be exaggerated. He is more powerful than any other Minister, and than most combinations of Ministers, but less powerful than the Cabinet collectively. The power of the Executive generally has increased, but this means that there are more departments and corporations to share that power; and the proliferation of committees means that information and influence are more widely distributed. In many ways the increase in Executive functions has made the task of supervision more difficult. Different aspects of policy and administration should be distinguished. The main influence of the Prime Minister lies in foreign policy, defence and national security, and in emergencies like the general strike, the abdication and the Rhodesian U.D.I. In economic policy his influence varies. He does not usually dabble in such matters as education or housing.

The extreme view, expressed in Humphry Berkeley's *The Power of the Prime Minister*, is that we have reached the stage of 'Presidential Government'. This view has less to commend it. There may be ways in which the Prime Minister has more actual power within this country than an American President; for example, he can bring about the dissolution of the Legislature, and his appointments do not require the approval of the Second Chamber. Yet the Presidential system–if by that we mean the American Presidential system–is so different from our own that comparison is difficult. In the first place the President is a directly elected head of State. Then he is not a member of the Legislature and is not responsible to it. He neither needs its support to continue in office, nor can he rely on a majority in either House to get his legislation passed. Moreover the fixed term of the President's office, and the fixed terms of Congressional elections, are in complete contrast to the continuing dependence of the Prime Minister on his party majority in the House of Commons, and his ability to manipulate the timing of Parliamentary elections. The differences between the Presidential and Congressional system on the one hand and our system of responsible Parliamentary government on the other, make it impracticable to adopt Mr. Berkeley's suggestion that the Prime Minister's term of office should be limited to two terms or a maximum of eight years. The transplant would be rejected by the body politic.

3

Parliament: the House of Commons

THE HOUSE OF COMMONS IS NOT PARLIAMENT

The House of Commons is so far the predominating partner in Parliament that there is a tendency – especially among members who are called 'Members of Parliament' – to regard the Commons as equivalent to Parliament. But Acts are passed by the Queen in Parliament, and this (subject to the Parliament Acts) requires the consent of both Houses. Since by Parliamentary custom, privilege and constitutional convention the Lords have no concern with national finance, this attitude has led at times to resolutions of the Commons, or of a Committee of the Commons, being regarded as if they were law. And so in *Bowles* v. *Bank of England* (1913) Gibson Bowles M.P. successfully challenged the legality of the deduction of income tax from interest accruing to him at the Bank of England on the authority of resolutions of the Committee of Ways and Means and in anticipation of the passing of the annual Finance Act. Although this was shown to have been the practice for more than a century, the Judge said it was a violation of the Bill of Rights, which declares that levying money for the use of the Crown without consent of Parliament is illegal. It is true that a Government can nearly always obtain the legal powers it wants, but this must be done, not by resolutions of the House but by Act of Parliament. This was in fact later done for this kind of case by the Provisional Collection of Taxes Act 1913, now replaced by the Act of 1968.

The temptation to treat resolutions of the House as law arises again in connection with Parliamentary privilege, discussed at the end of this chapter.

PARLIAMENT: THE HOUSE OF COMMONS

MEETING AND DURATION OF PARLIAMENT

One of the most remarkable features of our unwritten Constitution is that the central matters of the frequency and duration of Parliaments should be governed so little by law and so much by convention. These questions were very much in issue in the seventeenth century, but the only law our ancestors of that period left us on this topic consists of a declaration in the Bill of Rights that for the redress of all grievances and for the amending, strengthening and preserving of all laws, Parliament ought to be held 'frequently'; and the Meeting of Parliament Act 1694 which provided that a Parliament should be held once at least in three years, and that no Parliament should last more than three years. If we had a written Constitution it would provide that Parliament should be summoned at least once a year, and also that not more than one year should elapse between Parliamentary sessions. It would moreover be more explicit than our present practice as regards the duration of Parliament.

The maximum duration of Parliament, that is, its life period subject to earlier dissolution by prerogative, has been twice changed since 1694 for topical reasons. After the suppression of the Jacobite rising in 1715 the Duke of Devonshire on behalf of the Whigs introduced into the House of Lords a Bill that became the Septennial Act. This not only extended the maximum duration of future Parliaments to seven years, but prolonged the possible life of the existing Parliament as it was thought dangerous to hold a general election at that time. The effect of longer Parliaments was to strengthen the Ministry and the Commons against the King and the Lords. No Parliament in fact lasted longer than six years, and there were periods during the lifetime of this Act when the average duration of Parliaments was three or four years, but this only emphasises the significance of the prerogative in this context. We may notice that when a Parliament is dissolved, the House of Commons is dissolved in the sense that its members cease to be members; but the House of Lords is not dissolved, it continues in abeyance until the new Parliament is summoned.

It was part of the compromise whereby the Parliament Act 1911 was passed by the House of Lords that five years should be substituted for seven years as the time fixed for the maximum duration of Parliament under the Septennial Act 1715. (This came about through a clause which was discussed for less than one hour by the Commons.) It so happened that the Parliament which passed the Parliament Act 1911 prolonged its own life until the end of the first war by annual Acts, and Parliament acted in a similar way in the last war. As it is impracticable to hold a general election in wartime, there is no objection to what was done on those occasions.

A Lords' amendment to the Parliament Bill was accepted whereby 'a Bill containing any provision to extend the maximum duration of Parliament beyond five years' was expressly excluded from the provisions of section 2 limiting the Lords' power to delay the passing of Public Bills other than Money Bills. This ex-exception was obviously intended to be effective. It would be quite undemocratic as well as unconstitutional if the House of Commons could prolong its own life from time to time or indefinitely- becoming less and less representative of the people-by getting this exception repealed or by-passed by means of the procedure of the Parliament Act itself (as possibly amended in 1949). Yet this is just what a constitutional expert has recently suggested could be done. Basing himself on the sovereignty of Parliament and the principles that Parliament can repeal or amend any provision of an Act of Parliament either expressly or by implication and that the Courts have no jurisdiction to review legislation, Professor Denys Holland has argued that the Commons could secure the prolongation of the life of Parliament, without the consent of the Lords, under the machinery of the Parliament Act(s). He may be right. Who knows? The fact that the point could be seriously mooted in the correspondence columns of *The Times*, and that we cannot definitely say he is wrong, reinforces the argument put later in this book that the fundamentals of our Constitution need to be thoroughly examined and revised, and then enacted and entrenched.

DISSOLUTION OF PARLIAMENT AGAIN

This brings us again to the crucial question of the dissolution of Parliament. Within the maximum period laid down by the Parliament Act 1911 the Prime Minister can, as we have seen, advise the Queen to dissolve Parliament at any time, and she is generally expected to grant his request. Apart from the point, already made, that advice ought to come from the Cabinet as a body and not from the Prime Minister personally, what are the conventions and what is the practice? Convention would prevent the Queen from dissolving without or against the advice of her Ministers, even if it were not for the fact that proclamations and writs for summoning a new Parliament and holding elections would require the use of the Great Seal, which could not be done without the Lord Chancellor, a member of the Cabinet. On the converse question whether convention now requires the Queen in all cases to grant a dissolution when requested, opinion is divided. The 'new' doctrine is that the Sovereign no longer has any discretion in the matter: she must accept the advice of the Prime Minister; this is a clear and simple rule that keeps her out of the political arena. Some who adopt this doctrine would make an exception of the case where the Prime Minister asked for a second dissolution immediately after being defeated in a general election, provided that an alternative Government could be formed. The older, and we think the better, opinion is that there is no convention that the Queen must accede to every request for a dissolution, provided there are other Ministers who are prepared to carry on the Government, although a refusal nowadays would be very rare. This was the advice given by Lord Cave, former Lord Chancellor, to the King's private secretary when Ramsay MacDonald was leader of a minority Labour Government in 1923–24, and the opinion expressed by Viscount Simon in 1950 when Attlee's Labour Government was returned to the Commons with a majority of only six. The practice, or supposed convention, of granting a request to dissolve developed along with the two-party system. If that system broke up, as it has occasionally shown signs

51

of doing, different considerations would arise, because the acceptance of Ministers' advice is based on the assumption that they represent the wishes of the majority of the Commons and the electorate.

The practice is for the Prime Minister (formerly, as we have seen, the Cabinet) before the end of the statutory period of five years, after consulting his party henchmen and nowadays the public opinion polls, to choose a date for the dissolution – published as short a time as possible beforehand – that he thinks will be most advantageous to the Government party and most disadvantageous to the Opposition party. Since the Prime Minister and his fellow conspirators alone know when that date will be, they can juggle with direct and indirect taxes and manipulate the economy in such a way as to favour their chances at the general election. Any unpopular measures will have been taken in the earlier part of their term of office. This squalid practice of the leaders of both main parties as it has developed is the least creditable aspect of the British Constitution.

FIXED PARLIAMENTS, PHASED ELECTIONS OR SHORTER LIFE?

Formerly the justification of a Ministry's asking the Sovereign to dissolve Parliament was to get a fresh mandate from the people because either the Commons, being less bound than now by party, would not pass specific legislation or grant supplies, or the Lords frustrated the Government's legislative programme. The strengthening of party ties in the Commons and the restriction of the power of the Lords by the Parliament Acts have removed most of the justification for the use of dissolution as a political weapon. In addition to concentrating too much power in the hands of one person and giving the Government of the day an unfair advantage at a general election, our present practice introduces an element of uncertainty into the tenure of Members' seats. One remedy suggested by Humphry Berkeley and Ronald Butt (among others) is that there should be a statutory fixed term for the life of Parliament. Not much thought seems to have been given to the duration of the fixed term, which is usually assumed to be five years. A Prime Minister who commanded a majority in the Commons would not be entitled to ask for a dissolution before the expiry of the fixed term. Some see a danger in the prospect of a Government continuing in office after it had lost the confidence of the House, but the law as well as the convention would be that a Prime Minister who was defeated on a vote of confidence would be required to resign. Some restriction would have to be placed on what could properly be regarded as a motion of confidence, and it has been suggested that it should be confined to Finance Bills. A dissolution would then only follow if no other member of any party could obtain a vote of confidence. To this it may be objected that it might perpetuate a weak Government, and that the analogy to the American Constitution is false since the President is able to govern without a majority in Congress.

Another suggestion is that a certain proportion of the members of the Commons should be elected at fixed intervals – for example, every two years one-third of the members would be elected for a term of six years. Parliament would be permanent: there would be no dissolutions and no general elections. This proposal of phased or staggered elections would provide for continuity of experience in the House. It would also make the House a closer reflection of public opinion, which the scheme for a fixed-term Parliament (unless it was a fairly short term) would not do. Biennial elections, it is also argued, would avoid inflated majorities like those of 1945, 1959 and 1966, which tend to encourage arrogance in the Government party. The proposal could be fitted in with periodic elections, direct or indirect, to parts of the Second Chamber.

The main objection to the proposal for a fixed-term Parliament or for biennial elections is that it is not easily compatible with our system of responsible government. This is obvious with regard to fixed-term Parliaments. If we had biennial elections to a third of the seats, the Prime Minister and his colleagues would not be able to plan their policy more than about eighteen months ahead with any assurance that they would be able to see it through. The remedies proposed are too violent for the disease, serious though it is.

Our present evils–manipulation of the legislative programme and the economy and the timing of a general election to suit the advantage of the Government party, and a Government representing the people less and less the longer its period of office continues –could be largely mitigated by reducing the *maximum* duration of Parliament. In these days of instant communications by press, radio and television, and rapid change of events and opinions, five years (less such time as the Prime Minister finds convenient) is too long a period to wait between general elections. What would be the optimum term? On this there is no general agreement. Most countries with comparable political systems will probably be found to have settled on four years, though some have chosen three. From time to time since the Septennial Act was passed Parliament has been invited to revert to triennial elections. In Australia, where the maximum period is three years, there is a strong bias against intermediate dissolutions. In New Zealand the maximum period was reduced from five to three years in 1879; a quadrennial Act was passed in 1931 but in 1935 the triennial system was restored. There the practice is to dissolve *shortly* before the statutory date so as to fit in with such matters as harvest and holidays, but fixing the date of dissolution is not used as a political weapon. Only once since 1884 has the New Zealand Parliament been prematurely dissolved.

A common objection to the three-year period is that it is too short–the first year is spent in recovering from the last election, the third year is spent preparing for the next election, and only in the second year is any real work done. If, in spite of Australasian experience to the contrary, this argument is thought to be conclusive with respect to the greater complexity of the matters confronting the United Kingdom Parliament, then we could settle for a maximum period of four years. This would give the Prime Minister (or the Cabinet, if we revert to the former convention) with a serious programme to get through, much less scope than now for electioneering manoeuvres.

PARLIAMENT: THE HOUSE OF COMMONS

One might have thought that the Parliamentary franchise was one of the most important constitutional issues, and that any change in the voting age would be publicly canvassed as virtually a constitutional amendment. When we recall the furore over the Reform Acts in the nineteenth century and the militant activities of the Suffragettes at the turn of this century, leading first to a cautious grant of the franchise to women of thirty and culminating in the 'flapper' vote at twenty-one, we would expect a certain amount of public discussion of the idea of universal suffrage at eighteen. The right to vote was not even put forward as one of the students' 'demands'. In fact the latest extension of the franchise to several million electors (including resident Irish citizens) between the ages of eighteen and twenty-one took place by a sidewind. Interest had been aroused in the law requiring the parents' consent to a person marrying under the age of twenty-one, the minimum age for capacity to marry being sixteen. This led to a general consideration of the age of legal majority, and this question (not, by the way, including criminal law) was put to the Latey Committee. The age of 21 for majority was found to obtain in the largest number of countries, but the Latey Committee recommended a lowering of the age to eighteen for the purposes of parental consent, property and contract. The Commons, having properly reserved to themselves the question of the Parliamentary franchise, then set up an all-party Conference under the chairmanship of the Speaker. This Conference in 1968 recommended by 24 votes to one that the minimum age for voting should be reduced to twenty. The Cabinet decided, however, to introduce legislation lowering the voting age to eighteen before the next general election, and this was done by the Representation of the People Act 1969. If this gives the age-group concerned a greater sense of political responsibility and the feeling of 'belonging' to society, it may be for the best, but it was a curious way to go about it. No change was made to the minimum age for being elected to the House of

Commons: the Commons have not invited the eighteen-year-olds to sit with them.

ELECTORAL LAWS

The core of our electoral system is voting by secret ballot and a free choice of candidates. Secret voting was introduced by the Ballot Act 1872 to replace the hustings which left the field open for undue influence, bribery, corruption and intimidation. 'The ballot of each voter', stated the Act of 1872, 'shall consist of a paper . . . showing the names and description of the candidates. Each ballot shall have a number printed on the back, and shall have attached a counterfoil with the same number printed on the face. At the time of voting, the ballot paper shall be marked on both sides with an official mark, and delivered to the voter within the polling station, and the number of such voter on the register of voters shall be marked on the counterfoil, and the voter having secretly marked his vote on the paper, and folded it up so as to conceal his vote, shall place it in a closed box in the presence of the officer presiding at the polling station.' The Act went on to provide that after the close of the poll the ballot boxes should be sealed up and taken charge of by the returning officer who, in the presence of the candidates' agents, should open the boxes and ascertain the result of the poll. Every officer and agent must maintain the secrecy of the voting in the station, and he may not communicate, except for some purpose authorised by law, any information as to the name of any elector who has or has not applied for a ballot paper; and no person may interfere with a voter when marking his vote, or attempt to obtain in the polling station information as to the candidate for whom any voter is about to vote or has voted. No person may attempt to ascertain at the counting the number on the back of any ballot paper. The present law, contained in the Representation of the People Act 1949, is substantially similar. After the counting the ballot boxes are sealed and kept for a time in the Victoria Tower at the Houses of Parliament, and they may only be opened with the authority of a High Court Judge in connection with an election petition.

The deposit payable by a candidate, which is only forfeited if he fails to obtain one eighth of the votes, discourages frivolous nominations, but it is not true to say that it prevents the nomination of serious candidates – many people are willing to pay as much for a Hi-Fi set. The Speaker's Conference in 1968 made a number of recommendations concerning the law of Parliamentary elections, apart from the voting age. These included one that election broadcasts should be exempted from the statutory limitation on a candidate's expenditure. This will obviate such cases as *Grieve* v. *Douglas-Home* (1964), in which the Communists claimed that the election of Sir Alec Douglas-Home, then Conservative leader, was void as he had not included in his return of expenses the party political broadcasts made on behalf of the Conservative party. In that case it was held by an Election Court that no corrupt or illegal practice had been committed, as the motive of the B.B.C. was to give information to the public and not to promote Sir Alec's election. But the Government rejected two interesting recommendations of the Speaker's Conference: one, which had much to commend it, was that publication of opinion polls and betting odds within three days of a poll should be prohibited on the ground that they could influence voters unduly. The other, on which the arguments are more evenly balanced, was that the identification of the candidates' parties on nomination and ballot papers should continue to be prohibited. So the Representation of the People Act 1969 amends the rule that nomination and ballot papers may not refer to a candidate's political activities, by providing that they may contain a description not exceeding six words. This raises the question, who is to determine disputes concerning the way in which candidates describe themselves? In particular, who will arbitrate between the constituency party organisation and a breakaway candidate from the same party?

When a seat in the House becomes vacant through death or otherwise, any member by law may move that a writ to hold a by-election shall be issued, and polling must take place from 11 to 20 days after the issue of the writ, but no member is obliged to move the issue of a writ during the lifetime of a Parliament. The practice or custom–one can hardly flatter it with the name 'convention'–has arisen that when Parliament is in session the by-election writ should be moved in the House by a member of the party that previously held the seat. When Parliament is in recess any two members may instruct the Speaker to issue a warrant for a new writ, but this would be contrary to practice or custom. Thus a Government that is losing by-elections is able to postpone the issue of writs for an unreasonable time. Writs for by-elections for five Labour-held seats were issued on October 13, 1969, one of which had been vacant since February 19 and another since March 7. There obviously ought to be a statutory time-limit for the issue of a writ after a seat becomes vacant. In New Zealand the Speaker 'as soon as conveniently may be' directs the Clerk of the Writs to issue the Writ 'as soon as reasonably practicable' and not later than 21 days after receipt of the warrant.

ELECTORAL BOUNDARIES

An Electoral Boundaries Commission is a common feature in the Constitutions of Commonwealth countries. Each of the four parts of the United Kingdom has an independent Boundary Commission set up by the House of Commons (Redistribution of Seats) Acts 1949 and 1958, with the Speaker as chairman and judges as deputy chairmen. Periodical reviews of constituencies are to be made at intervals of ten to fifteen years with a view to recommending a redistribution of seats in accordance with population changes. The criteria the Commissions are expected to apply are not only numerical equality of voters in the various constituencies but also natural boundaries, the distance between parts of the same constituency, and the balance between the several parts of the United Kingdom. The Home Secretary is to lay the report before Parliament as soon as may be, together with a draft Order in Council giving effect to it. The Bill introduced by Mr. Callaghan, Home Secretary, in July 1969 implemented the Boundary Commission's recommendations with regard to Greater London (which happened to favour the Labour party) but not those with regard to the provinces (which happened to favour the Conservative party). The reason given was that Greater London government had recently been reformed, whereas local government in the provinces would be reformed in the 1970s following the Maud report; it was desirable that Parliamentary boundaries should coincide as far as practicable with local government boundaries, and undesirable that changes should be made at frequent intervals. The Bill laid the Government open to a charge of gerrymandering. Elections held with out-of-date boundaries would choose the Parliament that would have to decide how far to implement the Maud report. The Lords introduced a number of amendments to Mr. Callaghan's Bill, designed to bring it into line with the Commission's recommendations and so upholding constitutional principles; on the other hand the Lords in their turn laid themselves open to the criticism that they were interfering with representation in the Lower House. We may allow the Government the genuineness of its motives, and yet deplore the fact that it was able to appear to ride roughshod over constitutional provisions made twenty years ago with the intention of all parties that they should be beyond political intrigue. The dubiousness of the proceedings was not laid to rest by the Government's moving the closure in the Commons after a short debate in Committee, and imposing the Guillotine on subsequent discussion. When the Lords also rejected a revised version of the Bill, Mr. Callaghan announced that he would lay the required Orders before Parliament but advise his followers to reject them, which makes a mockery of the whole proceedings.

The electoral laws – universal adult suffrage, annual meeting of Parliament, periodic elections and secret ballot – which would be entrenched in most Constitutions, remain with us at the will of Parliament, which means at the will of a temporary majority in the House of Commons.

PARTICIPATION

The importance of preserving the integrity of our electoral system is that, with a population as large as ours, the only way in which the people can participate in government at the national level is by periodic elections. Direct government by initiative or referendum, as Laski wrote, is too crude for the purposes of modern government. Most questions cannot be framed in a suitable way. Complex matters of detail, as well as principle, need to be discussed, and proposals may require amendment. An undifferentiated electorate would have neither the interest nor the knowledge to make satisfactory decisions. Direct government is also incompatible with our responsible Parliamentary system. And popular opinion usually gives negative results. What is needed is the election of representatives who are informed and qualified to exercise judgment. The functions of the State, as Mr. Grimond has remarked, cannot be carried on at a continual public meeting. Consultation at an early stage of legislation with organised specialist interests, rather than interference by opinionated busybodies, is more to the point. 'Not "participation", but communication is the problem,' writes Professor Bernard Crick: 'we are obsessed with the idea of "democracy" as direct participation–as if we lived in the *Polis* of Athens, the Rochdale Co-op or the Carlton Club, or else with perfecting representative institutions as the next best thing in a world that has most unfortunately grown too large for direct participation. But we are only at the beginning of seeing democracy as communication'. We may not be able to perfect representative institutions but, as we have suggested, we could improve them by shortening the maximum period between general elections.

SELECTION OF CANDIDATES

Among the criticisms commonly made about the House of Commons at the present day is the allegation, which many are prepared to deny, that the quality of members has declined since before the war. Whether this is so or not, the quality of members must be affected in some degree by the methods of selecting candidates for election. The usual method is selection for nomination by a small committee of the constituency party organisation. If it is a safe seat, the selected candidate will be elected, and may continue as the member for many years. This applies not only to the original selection, but to the re-selection of sitting members at subsequent general elections. However suitable the candidates nominated may be, how do we know that many better persons may not have been available? Hence arose the suggestion that our political parties might borrow from American experience the system of primary elections, in which all the supporters of a party in the constituency could take part in the choice. This, it is claimed, would have the additional advantage of giving the candidate or member a more representative body in his constituency to whom he could appeal if he quarrelled with the local party committee or the party Whips. Primaries have in fact already been tried out by the Conservatives at Reigate in 1968 and Wimbledon in 1969, though it is too soon to say whether the scheme is likely to be successful. So far the meeting at which short-listed candidates spoke briefly and answered questions, and the vote was taken, has been attended by only about 10 per cent of the paid-up party members. The main drawback, however, is that the short-list of candidates was prepared by a small committee. At Wimbledon, where 340 persons applied, a selection committee of 14 interviewed 31 candidates and chose a short list of three; but at least the meeting of members had three to choose from, instead of merely being asked to endorse one; and a primary election does allow a wider range of party opinion to be brought to bear.

RIGIDITY OF THE PARTY SYSTEM

The rigidity of the party system is one of the factors blamed for the present predicament of private members, and for the alleged decline in public respect for Parliament generally. On the one hand our Parliamentary institutions as they have developed in modern times presuppose the party system. 'It will generally be found,' wrote Sir Ivor Jennings, 'that the critic who asserts that parties are unnecessary has a belief in the rightness of his own opinion so profound that he does not realise that it is a partisan opinion. . . . The true democrat has a suspicion that he may not always be right.' A majority that is tolerant of minority opinions appears to be the best, if not the only, way to decide broad issues. But opinions based on interest change from time to time. 'Majorities are unstable, and the Opposition of today is the Government of tomorrow.' This fact reconciles the minority to submitting for a time to the policy of the majority. The two-party system suits our institutions best, for the main difference between the parties is not so much a difference of aims as about the speed with which, and the methods by which, the country should move towards its goal. The House of Commons must be organised for action. Without party there would be no stability, for a Government would have no assurance of a majority in the House from one day to the next. Yet the very meaning of 'Parliament' is discussion, and convention prevents a Government from simply using its majority to push through its measures without debate.

On the other hand the party system as operated in the Commons can become unnecessarily rigid. The Whips tend to be put on for divisions on almost every Government measure, however non-vital. They are hard task-masters, especially to Labour members. Conservative members perhaps suffer more from their constituency organisations. There is a growing body of opinion that 'votes of confidence' are exaggerated. One example was the imposition of a three-line Whip in the debate on the controversial proposal to make the pound rather than ten shillings the basic unit of our projected decimal currency. That episode also illustrated another recent trend, the holding of the genuine debate in a private meeting of party members (misleadingly called a party 'Parliamentary committee') in advance of a dragooned debate in the House. This practice is seen as another cause of the depressed status of private members and the 'decline of Parliament'. Another instance was the meetings held by the Parliamentary Labour party on the Common Market negotiations in 1967, imparting information that would be more properly given in a White Paper which could be debated in the House.

With regard to the exaggeration of motions of confidence, there is no good reason why—apart from really vital matters like finance—the Government should not be expected to drop a defeated Bill and carry on. The Government might even do this, in spite of the defection of some of its members, with the help of the Opposition, which does not at all times want to turn a Government out. One peccadillo need not necessarily indicate the irretrievable breakdown of the marriage between the Commons and the Government.

Another consequence of the strict party discipline enforced by the Whips, according to some writers, is that the real curb on the Government has passed from the Opposition to the Government backbenchers. Even when the Government's majority is small, it is enough to carry the day. The Opposition cannot exert a check on the Government, it can only protest. Government backbenchers, on the other hand, can show their dissatisfaction by abstaining or occasionally voting against the Government, and by criticism in the party Parliamentary committee.

There are signs that the grip of the party machine has in fact been relaxed somewhat on both sides of the House during the 1960s, except when the 1964 Labour Government had a very small majority. This significant reversal may be due to the fact that the House has recruited a larger proportion of young and active members.

ROLE OF THE PRIVATE MEMBER

Since the abolition of the University franchise against the recommendation of a Speaker's Conference in 1948, and the replacement of the amateur by the professional politician, the independent member of the House of Commons has virtually become extinct. Electors vote for the party rather than the man. Only in marginal constituencies does the personality of a candidate have any appreciable effect on the result. Although a member still represents his constituency in the sense that he takes up the grievances of his constituents regardless of party, as a voting member of the House he is (with rare and temporary exceptions) a piece of the party machine. While Labour members are kept in line mainly by the party whip, Conservative members are curbed more by their constituency party Associations. Following their criticism of the Suez campaign in 1956, Sir Frank Medlicott and

Mr. Nigel Nicolson (who also favoured the abolition of the death penalty) were not re-adopted by their constituencies, and Mr. Anthony Nutting, who resigned as Minister of State at the Foreign Office, was induced to relinquish his seat.

Ever since the Reform Act 1832 there has been a tendency for the Government to monopolise the time of the House at the expense of private members. A limited number of Fridays and a very few other days are now allotted to private members, who have to ballot for priority in the time available. They are not restricted as regards subject-matter of legislation, except that they do not introduce Bills authorising expenditure since they would require Government support for a financial resolution after second reading; but unless the Government gives a private member's Bill its active support it is unlikely to reach an advanced stage before the end of the session. It has been suggested that a steering committee would be an improvement over merely waiting on the luck of the draw, or that priority should be given to private members' Bills according to the amount of support they obtain in the House. It is commonly stated that there is less time than formerly allotted to private members, but examination seems to show that members in the nineteenth century used the greater amount of time at their disposal in making lengthier speeches, indulging in longer debates and asking questions as and when they chose. Outstanding examples of successful efforts have been A. P. Herbert's Matrimonial Causes Act 1937 (which also attempted to revive the informative preamble) and Mr. Silverman's Murder (Abolition of Death Penalty) Act 1965. In fact the period since 1964 has been notable for the enactment of private members' Bills affecting the life of society in such fields as homosexual offences, abortion and the censorship of stage plays. Whether one approves of the impact of this kind of legislation will depend on how far one is willing to go along with permissiveness. The Government have helped by allowing time, but have neither assisted with the drafting nor accepted responsibility for the policies.

When we recall that backbenchers in the 1968–69 session compelled the Government to drop House of Lords reform (which figured prominently in the Queen's Speech) in favour of its incomes policy, and then compelled it to drop its 'essential' incomes policy in favour of a Bill imposing legal sanctions against trade unions, and finally compelled it to drop legal sanctions against trade unions – all laudable legislative policies in their way – we can hardly say that backbenchers have no role left except to be lobby-fodder or Ombudsmen for their constituents.

Another reason given for the depressed state of private members is the inadequate conditions of service under which they labour. The present complaint is not about salaries. The pay of members who are not Ministers has been increased from time to time and is now £3,250 per annum. They receive travelling allowances, an expenses allowance up to £750 per annum and free postage to government departments and nationalised industries. Comparison with the offices and secretarial assistance provided for American Congressmen is misleading because fact-finding is a great part of their business, whereas in our system most of the required information can be obtained either by questions in the House or by writing to the department. Yet it is generally agreed that more should be done for our members. This is not a constitutional issue, but merely a matter of being willing to find the money. Something more is in fact being done because a Select Committee on services and facilities for members recommended in July 1969 that members should be granted certain concessions and extra allowances to help them to meet out-of-pocket expenses for secretarial services, telephone calls and postage. It recommended that provision should be made at public expense for secretarial assistance, or an allowance to meet the cost of one full-time secretary per member. Free trunk calls have been agreed by the Treasury.

REFORM OF LEGISLATIVE PROCEDURE

We hear so many criticisms nowadays expressing the view that Parliament has become ineffective, or that we ought to devise ways of making Parliament more effective, that we may well ask the question: effective for what purpose? It is a misapprehension to suppose either that it is the aim of a good legislature to pass as many laws as possible in a given time, or that Parliament should try to govern the country. Although we use the expression 'Parliamentary government', we really mean government by the Executive in Parliament. The proper office of a representative assembly, wrote J. S. Mill in his *Representative Government*, instead of the function of governing, for which it is radically unfit, is to watch and control the government, to be at once the nation's Committee of Grievances and its Congress of Opinions. The critics tend to exaggerate the extent to which Parliament controlled the Government in the past. We do read of Prime Ministers losing their support, Governments being defeated and Bills being redrafted in the House in the nineteenth century, but since the Reform Act 1867 we have hardly been able to say that it is the Commons who make and unmake Governments. There are some Constitutions in which the Prime Minister is elected by the legislative assembly, but the British Prime Minister is accepted, not appointed, by Parliament. Parliament insists that the general policy of the Government should meet with its approval; it then grants the Government the powers and funds needed to carry out that policy within the law. Our system of Ministerial responsibility to Parliament also does much to prevent corruption and to restrain injustice.

The procedure on legislation, much of which is unwritten practice, is entirely within the control of the House itself. The main purpose of making Standing Orders has been to speed up debate. What is contained in a Standing Order or a sessional order can be changed by an order of the same kind, and either can be suspended by an *ad hoc* order. The Speaker or Chairman of Committee gives rulings interpreting the orders and practice of the House, and applies them to particular circumstances as they arise. There is probably no other country in which the authority of the Speaker as impartial chairman and defender of the rights of minorities has been developed to such a high degree. The Government with its majority inevitably controls Parliamentary time and has a majority on all committees. Convention requires that the time available should be allotted fairly to the various measures and stages of legislation and that closures, guillotines and kangaroos should be imposed after consultation with the other side. This at any rate is the theory; but the time available depends on the amount of legislation the Government chooses to introduce, and the sanction is the prospect of the Government and the Opposition changing places after the next general election. A Government that twisted the rules too much to suit its own convenience might find the blows returned with interest when the roles have been reversed.

A stream of reports has come in recent years from Select Committees on Procedure. Arising out of their recommendations and the reforming zeal of Mr. Crossman when Leader of the House, a number of important reforms in the legislative process have been made. According to the Procedure Committee of 1966–67 the aims are to streamline the legislative process, for the House to make better use of time by attempting to achieve a more balanced debate of the details of Bills in committee and on report, and by involving itself at an earlier stage in the preparation of certain kinds of legislation. Mr. Crossman's aims were to relieve pressure on the floor of the House, to restore it as the forum of the nation's political debate, to make public Bill procedure more efficient, to obviate all-night sittings, and at the same time to strengthen the control of the Executive by the House.

Morning sittings were introduced as an experiment, although many members are engaged on committee work in the mornings and others carry on outside occupations. Sittings were held on Monday and Wednesday mornings for minor business, such as Statutory Instruments and non-contentious Bills. After a time the experiment was abandoned as a failure, in exchange for a Standing Order allowing a Minister to move a motion that a debate continuing after 10 p.m. be suspended until the following morning.

Second Reading Committees have been a more successful experiment, and are now provided for by Standing Order. A Bill may go to a Second Reading Committee of 20 to 80 members, unless twenty members rise in their places to object. Bills of secondary importance may also be sent to a Standing Committee at report stage.

The 1966–67 Procedure Committee doubted whether too much time was spent on the Finance Bill, but recommended voluntary time-tabling, which was accepted by the Government as an experiment: if agreement failed, then after a two-hour debate a time-table would be imposed. There were suggestions that this procedure might be extended to all public Bills. The experiment of a voluntary time-table broke down, and the 1968 Budget was debated in Committee. The Finance Bill was sent to a Standing Committee of 50 members, and the time-honoured Committees of Ways and Means and of Supply – Committees of the whole House – disappeared.

The Select Committee on Procedure, 1968–69, recommended that an Expenditure White Paper should be published each November, which should be debated by the House for two days, in addition to any debates held on Supply days. From November onwards a Select Committee on Expenditure and about eight Sub-Committees (to replace the Estimates Committee) would conduct inquiries and publish reports for consideration by the Government and the House before the next Expenditure debate in the autumn. Only about 40 members bothered to attend the debate on the first White Paper in January 1970.

Voluntary time-tabling has been extended in committee and on report, with the Government's 'reserve power' in the background.

Third reading debates, which tended to be repetitive, have now become mainly formal. Debate is only permitted on a motion supported by at least six members. It is therefore for the first time possible for some Bills to pass without ever being debated on the floor of the House.

The Select Committee on Procedure 1966–67 recommended that regular use should be made of *ad hoc* committees to study and report on specific topics of possible legislation referred to them. There is support for pre-legislative committees, to be consulted before legislation is prepared and even preparing some non-controversial Bills themselves. This would do something to meet the complaint that outside interests are consulted by Ministers before Bills are finally drafted, but not members of Parliament themselves, who are faced with a *fait accompli*.

Criticism has often been made of the rule that all public Bills (including private members' Bills) in progress were killed by the prorogation of Parliament. The rule was defended by the argument that it is better that Parliament should clear its books at the end of a session than that stale Bills should clutter the Order Paper next session. Prorogation, it is said, keeps the Government up to the mark in the attempt to complete its legislative programme. Anyway, a Minister may be content to drop a poorly drafted Bill and to introduce an improved version later. The 1966–67 Procedure Committee suggested that certain Bills should be carried over from one session to the next, namely, Bills that have been considered by a Second Reading Committee, unless the motion to carry them over is opposed by twenty members rising in their places.

A perennial suggestion is that there should be a time-limit for member's speeches, (say) twenty minutes for the front bench and ten minutes for backbenchers. Certainly, if one reads Hansard one marvels at the amount of repetition and that some members can take so long to say so little. New Zealand introduced a time-limit on speeches in the House as long ago as 1895. The custom of giving priority to Privy Councillors in debate is also unpopular with backbenchers.

Proxy voting for sick members has a fair measure of support.

SCRUTINY OF ADMINISTRATION: SUGGESTED REFORMS

Parliamentary procedure has been described as antiquated, time-wasting and incomprehensible, with its all-night sittings and the use of Supply time to discuss foreign affairs. Recent reforms have benefited Ministers rather than private members. They have helped the Government to get their business through more speedily, but have done little to help members to keep a check on the Executive. The most important innovation has been, in a sense, extra-Parliamentary, that is the appointment of the Parliamentary Commissioner for Administration, commonly known as the

Ombudsman, who will be discussed in chapter 6.

Most politicians and academic writers have advocated a more extensive use of committees, though there has been a diversity of opinion as to whether they should be Standing Committees or *ad hoc* or Sessional Select Committees. It has been suggested by some that Standing or Select Committees attached to particular departments, with power to summon Ministers and civil servants and to call for papers, should deal with the second reading of Bills relating to the department concerned, regardless of the difference between the American or French political system and our own, where the function of examining and criticising important Government policy belongs to Parliament as a whole. The members could be elected by backbenchers of each party instead of being appointed by the Whips. Further, *ad hoc* committees set up as in the nineteenth century to investigate particular problems would return to the House of Commons the consideration of some subjects of a political nature now delegated to Committees of Enquiry and Royal Commissions. Again, it was hoped that, if the role of Parliament is seen as advising rather than controlling the Executive, Committees–in spite of the party affiliations of their members–would be capable of representing the national interest, a democratic influence against bureaucratic arbitrariness.

Professor Bernard Crick thinks that Parliament spends too much time on legislation, and not enough time on general debate and scrutiny of the administration. The main function of Parliament he sees as the publicising of key issues, 'alerting and informing the public on matters relevant to the decision which way (or whether) to vote'. In advocating an extended use of Standing Committees of Advice, Scrutiny and Investigation, he prefers to call them 'Specialized' rather than 'Specialist' Committees: a committee specialises in a particular field, but the members themselves are not specialists in that field. Governing has become a prolonged election campaign, and constitutional conventions are really the agreed devices by which the continuous election campaign of the whole life of Parliament is fought. It is not the electorate that influences Parliament which controls the Government, according to Bernard Crick, but Parliament that influences the electorate which controls the Government.

These Standing Committees would neither be like the American committees which 'control' the Executive, nor would they replace the existing Standing Committees which take the committee stage of Bills, but would rather resemble the Select Committees on Estimates, Public Accounts and Nationalised Industries. They would last the lifetime of a Parliament. Members would specialise on groups of departments or single departments, including the annual departmental Estimates. Ministers could use such committees as sounding-boards for future legislation, and as partners in investigating the efficiency of the administration.

Members with such diverse affiliations as Mr. G. R. Strauss and Mr. Angus Maude, on the other hand, have expressed reservations about Specialist Committees of the House. In the United States the Executive does not sit in Congress, so that its specialist committees are the only method by which their activities can be examined. Moreover the American President appears to be gaining power at the expense of Congress, so that it is probably illusory to suppose that Parliament would recover some of its authority if we extended the committee system. In most European countries there are coalition Governments, so that a spread of decision-making is unavoidable. With us, the Cabinet must initiate and determine the priority of legislation. A committee composed of members of opposing parties could not usefully participate in the preparation of Bills with whose objects they partly disagreed. If we did set up such committees their members over a period of time would assume a privileged position, and the result might be to diminish, rather than to increase, the responsibility of Ministers to Parliament.

Nearly all the advocates of Parliamentary reform emphasise the informative role of Parliament, and suggest that its influence on policy can most usefully be exerted through its advice to the Government on the quality of the administration. There is little support for the view that the Commons can directly influence the formation or modification of policy, either by the majority party exerting pressure on the Government or (still less) by the House as a whole representing public opinion. Mr. Ronald Butt, however, sees Parliament as guardian of the liberties of the subject and a safeguard against administrative abuses. He believes there is more to the Parliamentary process than a continuous election campaign. Specialised committees are admittedly useful for the oversight of the administration, but they are not a full answer because they could only function in uncontentious matters, such as health and welfare, and not in such matters as foreign and defence policy. And it would be a pity if absorption in administrative detail were to divert the attention of members of Parliament away from political issues. Mr. Butt is not alone in feeling the need to restore greater reality to debates on high policy, and to streamline procedure for this purpose.

SPECIALIST COMMITTEES AND OTHER REFORMS

The fourth Report from the Select Committee on Procedure 1964–65 suggested that a new Select Committee should be set up, as a development of the Estimates Committee, to examine how the departments carry out their responsibilities, and to consider their estimates of expenditure and reports. The Estimates Committee already made a wide review of government administration, but this new committee would go further and deeper. No change designed to increase the efficiency of the House of Commons as a debating chamber must be allowed to supersede the traditional right of the Commons to consider grievances before granting supply, nor to absolve them from their duty to examine government expenditure and administration. For this more information should be made available to members, so that when they take part in debates they may be armed with the necessary background knowledge. This requires that the House should possess a more efficient system of scrutiny of administration. In advocating the Select Committee system for this purpose, the Committee on Procedure sought to avoid disturbing the relationship of Ministers to Parliament, or instituting methods that might drain away interest from the proceedings of the House as a whole. It suggested that the new

Committee should function through Sub-Committees specialising in various spheres of governmental activity, each named according to its special subject. A Select Committee on Agriculture and another on Science and Technology were subsequently set up at the end of 1966 as a sessional experiment. The former was 'departmental', covering the activities of a department, and the latter 'functional', being confined to certain specific projects and problems. They were empowered to examine witnesses in public, and to appoint technical or scientific consultants. In the following year a Committee was set up to review the activities of the Department of Education and Science and the Scottish Education Department. Mr. Crossman said he hoped to set up two or more of these departmental committees each year until all domestic policy was subject to scrutiny. The last and most difficult hurdle would be foreign affairs and defence. Here it may be noted that the making of the nuclear bomb without consulting Parliament was possible because annual sums were voted for 'research'. It was suggested that committees dealing with housing and with trade and industry should be created in the 1967–68 session. But the intention, said Mr. Crossman, was that these committees should spend one session on each department and then move on. This statement came as a surprise, because members and others who had advocated the creation of such committees had envisaged that they would maintain a continuous scrutiny of the departments concerned.

The Select Committee on Agriculture–the only one at that time covering a department–was closed down early in 1969. The Select Committee on Education and Science, which did not endear itself to the University authorities in 1968–69, was renewed for a session and inquired into teacher training. Two new Committees were set up on the Scottish Office and on Overseas Aid. There are also committees watching over the working of the Race Relations Act and the Parliamentary Commissioner, but these are not scrutinies of government departments. Ministers and civil servants can hardly be expected to relish the criticism of departmental committees. The same applies to an Opposition front bench that looks to the future. Members conclude ruefully that

F 73

the Cabinet can create and abolish committees at will, and that there is nothing much the House can do to reform itself. Again one asks, is the aim of Parliamentary reform more legislation or better administration?

The White Paper on House of Lords Reform (November 1968), which preceded the introduction of the abortive Parliament (No. 2) Bill 1969, envisaged the reform of the House of Lords being followed by a more even spreading of Parliamentary work between the two Houses, not only in the introduction and consideration of Bills, but also by having members of both Houses on Specialist Committees, whether departmental, *ad hoc* or functional.

It used to be complained that the Prime Minister's Questions were not reached because of the number of Supplementaries asked of other Ministers. From 1961 a quarter of an hour has been set aside for the Prime Minister to answer Questions after 3.15 p.m. on Tuesdays and Thursdays; but now it is contended that the Prime Minister dominates Question time; policy questions cannot be answered satisfactorily except at length, and the set time gives the Prime Minister a regular platform from which to propound his views on current issues. Although Question Time is generally considered to be one of the most valuable defences of individual liberty, it has been described as a 'ritual exchange of non-information' (*Guardian*, July 10, 1964), in which civil servants, who prepare Ministers' answers, practise the art of concealment.

Some members stigmatise Adjournment debates and Questions as perfunctory and inadequate.

One recent improvement has been the redefinition of urgency motions under Standing Order No. 9. The old formula of 'a definite matter of urgent public importance' permitted fewer and fewer debates as it became overlaid with restrictive Speakers' rulings. Members may be more successful with the new definition: 'a specific and important matter that should have urgent consideration', although it is undesirable that debates under this Order should become too frequent.

PARLIAMENT: THE HOUSE OF COMMONS

The special branch of law relating to Parliamentary privilege is important, not only for the protection of Parliamentary government, but also in connection with the liberty of the citizen. Erskine May describes Parliamentary privilege as 'the sum of the peculiar rights enjoyed by each House collectively as a constituent part of the High Court of Parliament, and by members of each House individually, without which they could not discharge their functions, and which exceed those possessed by other bodies or individuals'. Privilege is part of the law and custom of Parliament, though some of it has statutory authority, notably the provision of the Bill of Rights 1688 that 'the freedom of speech or debates or proceedings in Parliament ought not to be impeached or questioned in any Court or place out of Parliament'. But the House of Commons has assumed and exercised powers, such as that of committing strangers to prison for contempts not amounting to obstruction of its proceedings, which are not essential to the discharge of its functions, because some kinds of contempt could be made offences triable by the ordinary Courts. So it was held by the Privy Council in *Kielley* v. *Carson* (1842) that the House of Assembly of Newfoundland had no power to punish (as distinct from ejecting) interrupters. The British Houses of Parliament had acquired this power for historical reasons as being part of the High *Court* of Parliament.

The two Houses have similar privileges, but the Upper House has seldom had occasion to come into conflict with the Sovereign or the Courts in this sphere. The privileges of the Commons against the Crown (freedom of speech in debate and the regulation of its own composition and internal proceedings) have been settled since 1688. Their privileges against the Lords are partly superseded by the Parliament Acts. It is their privileges against the individual citizen, and the manner of their exercise, that call for reform. Is a letter from a member to a Minister about some matter that is, or may come, before Parliament a 'proceeding in Parliament', so that a person defamed in the letter would have no right of action for libel? In the *Strauss* case (1958) the Committee of Privileges reported that such a letter was a proceeding in Parliament, and the injured party and their solicitors had committed a breach of privilege in threatening to issue a writ; but the House by a majority of five resolved that it was not–a decision that could be reversed by a vote of the House in any later case. The Commons have always tried to prevent any question of privilege being decided by the Courts, but they occasionally seek an advisory opinion from the Judicial Committee of the Privy Council as to the meaning of a relevant Act of Parliament. So in the *Strauss* case the Commons referred to the Judicial Committee the meaning of the Parliamentary Privilege Act 1770, which provides that it shall not be a breach of privilege for any person to bring an action in any Court against a member of either House. The opinion was that the Act applies only to proceedings against members in their *private* capacity, for example, actions for debt. After the general election of 1950 a Select Committee was set up to inquire into the eligibility to sit in the Commons of the Rev. J. G. MacManaway, a clergyman of the Church of Ireland. Owing to the complexity of the law the Select Committee was unable to reach a definite conclusion, and the House referred the question to the Judicial Committee, which advised that the disqualification attached to clergy who had been episcopally ordained.

The leading case on the regulation of the internal proceedings of the House is *Bradlaugh* v. *Gossett* (1884), in which Charles Bradlaugh, the well-known atheist who had been elected as member for Northampton, brought an action in the High Court against the Serjeant-at-Arms for an injunction to restrain him from forcibly excluding Bradlaugh from the House; and a declaration that the order of the House preventing him as an atheist from taking the member's statutory oath was void. Judgment was given for the Serjeant-at-Arms on the ground that these matters were covered by the privileges of the House; but Mr. Justice Stephen made it clear that, if the House had allowed Bradlaugh to sit and had then purported by resolution to protect him against any statutory penalties to which he might at that time have been liable *in the*

Courts at the suit of a common informer, the Court would not have allowed such resolution to prevent the recovery of the penalty.

One of the most important privileges is the power to punish persons, whether members or strangers, who commit a breach of privilege or contempt. 'Privileges', strictly speaking, are specific: the most important ones have been mentioned. The Lords passed a resolution in 1704, to which the Commons assented, that neither House has power to create for itself new privileges not warranted by the known laws and customs of Parliament. 'Contempt', on the other hand, is not defined but is determinable by the House.

Contempts generally are offences against the authority or dignity of the House, such as defamatory or disrespectful writings or statements about the House or its members as such, disobedience to the orders of the House, or obstructions to the business or officers of the House. Offences against the authority or dignity of the House cannot be enumerated, the power to punish for contempt being discretionary. A breach of privilege is also a contempt –indeed, the two terms are often used indiscriminately; but a contempt is not necessarily a breach of privilege. In *Allighan's Case* (1947) a member wrote a newspaper article stating that confidential information relating to Parliamentary party meetings was conveyed by members to newspapers, partly for payment and partly under the influence of drink. The Committee for Privileges found the general statement untrue, with the exception of Mr. Allighan himself and another member. The House resolved that there had not been a breach of privilege, but that Mr. Allighan had been guilty of contempts in writing the article and in the evasive manner in which he had answered the Committee. They also invented the offence of 'dishonourable conduct' in accepting payment for the disclosure of confidential information. Mr. Allighan was expelled from the House, and the editor of the paper was reprimanded for gross contempt.

There have been periods since the war when members of the House have been particularly touchy about their dignity. Complaints of contempt have been brought against journalists and other strangers for slight reason, although the House is sometimes

77

content with an apology and often decides to take no action, while reserving the right to do so. In the case of *Junor* (1957) a journalist published an article in the *Sunday Express* criticising members of Parliament for not having protested against the over-generous petrol ration allotted by statutory order to political parties in the constituencies at the time of the Suez crisis: members were accused of self-interest in failing to protest at the unfair discrimination in their favour. The House resolved that this was a serious contempt. They took no action beyond requiring Mr. Junor to apologise at the bar of the House, but even that is an acutely embarrassing experience. When a Sub-Committee of the Select Committee on Education and Science visited Essex University in 1969 to hear evidence on the relationship between students and their Universities and Colleges, their meeting had to be adjourned to a private room because of persistent interruption and obstruction on the part of members of the audience. The Committee of Privileges advised that this conduct disclosed a contempt of the House, but recommended that it was not an occasion on which the House should exercise its penal jurisdiction. They concluded that in general meetings of Select Committees had better be held in Westminster, where the Serjeant-at-Arms can control the situation, and that if it is expedient to hold a meeting outside the precincts and disorderly conduct is expected, the proceedings should not be in public.

The House can commit to prison by warrant of the Speaker for what it chooses to call breach of privilege or contempt. A member is committed to the Clock Tower, and a stranger is handed over to one of Her Majesty's prisons by the Serjeant-at-Arms, who may by statute call on the assistance of the Metropolitan Police. Although the Commons cannot commit beyond the end of the session, they may re-commit the person in the next session. When we consider that the House in such cases is judge in its own cause; that the accused has no right to be defended by counsel or to call witnesses; that there are no rules of evidence; that there is no jury to find the facts; that the truth, or a belief in the truth, is no defence (though it may mitigate punishment); that a denial of the charge may be held to aggravate the offence; and that there is no appeal—when we consider all this, we may question whether the House is subject to 'the rule of law'. The matter is made more serious by the fact—as we have seen in relation to the case of *Stockdale* v. *Hansard* (1839) in chapter 1—that the House claims exclusive jurisdiction to decide not only the manner in which its privileges shall be exercised, but also the question whether or not a given case is covered by privilege.

The Commons finally gave up to the Courts their right to determine disputed elections by the Parliamentary Elections Act 1868 (now replaced by the Representation of the People Act 1949). In the same way the two Houses could by an Act of Parliament transfer to the Courts the jurisdiction to deal with cases concerning privilege or contempt, while reserving for themselves sufficient power to enable them to maintain order in the House. This could be accompanied by a clearer definition of both 'privilege' and 'contempt'; offences which would thereafter be kept within proper bounds by the Courts, with all the other safeguards to the citizen of judicial procedure.

A Select Committee on Parliamentary Privilege was appointed in 1966 to review the law of Parliamentary privilege as it affects the House of Commons and the procedure by which cases of privilege are raised and dealt with in the House, and to report whether any changes in the law or practice were desirable. The Committee's report, published at the end of 1967, recommended extensive changes which would meet some of the criticisms that have been made. The first recommendation was that the expression 'Parliamentary Privilege' should cease to be used; that the House should speak of its 'rights and immunities', and of 'contempt' rather than 'breach of privilege'. In this the Committee seem to have gone too far to avoid giving the impression that members are, or desire to be, a 'privileged class' for, as we have seen, 'privileges' are capable of being precisely defined whereas the subject-matter of 'contempt' is not. The other main recommendations are that: (1) The House should exercise its penal jurisdiction as sparingly as possible, and only when the House is satisfied that to exercise it is essential for the reasonable protection of the House, its members or officers from obstruction or substantial interference with the performance of its functions; (2) In the ordinary case where a member has a remedy in the Courts, for example in defamation, he should not be permitted to invoke the penal jurisdiction of the House; (3) Trivial complaints should be dismissed summarily without investigation; (4) The truth, or reasonable belief in the truth of allegations, should be taken into account in considering whether contempt has been committed; (5) Legislation should be passed to extend and clarify the scope of the defences of absolute and qualified privilege available in the Courts to actions brought against Ministers and others; for example, absolute privilege should cover things said or done in the Chamber or during proceedings (within the precincts) of a Committee of the House, documents authorised by the House, Questions and Notices of Motion, and communications between members and certain other persons (the decision of the House in the *Strauss Case* to be reversed); while qualified privilege (which is a defence only in the absence of malice) would cover other communications connected with a member's Parliamentary functions; (6) Legislation should abolish impeachment, which can only be initiated by the Commons and has been regarded as obsolete since the early nineteenth century; (7) The rules regarding the admission of the public to the House and to Committees, the reporting of proceedings of the House and of Committees, and the publication of evidence given before Select Committees should be modified; (8) (*a*) Complaints of contempt should no longer be made to the Speaker in the Chamber, except in the case of improper or disorderly conduct taking place in the Chamber itself or a gallery or lobby; but a member should raise his complaint 'as promptly as is reasonably practicable' to the Clerk to the Committee of Privileges (to be called the 'Select Committee of House of Commons Rights'); (*b*) The Committee, usually acting through a small Sub-Committee, would decide the preliminary question whether there is a *prima facie* case to justify full investigation by the Committee; (*c*) If the matter is fully investigated the

Committee (instead of the Leader of the House, as now) should recommend to the House the appropriate penalty; (9) Persons against whom a complaint is made should be entitled to attend, and to apply for representation by a lawyer or any other person; and the Committee should be able to permit, or refuse permission for, the calling of witnesses, with the attendant rights of examination, cross-examination and re-examination, and of making submissions; (10) Legislation should enable the Committee to authorise legal aid; and (11) Legislation should empower the House of Commons to impose fines and fixed periods of imprisonment.

These recommendations not only go a long way to meet the criticisms of Parliamentary privilege and the manner in which it is enforced by the House of Commons, but (if adopted) they should also make conflicts between the House and the Courts less likely.

4

Parliament: the Second Chamber

COMPOSITION OF THE HOUSE OF LORDS

Our institutions often retain their antique appearance long after their actual function in society has changed, and such functional changes as they have undergone are the product of experience rather than theory. This is true of the House of Lords as it is of the Monarchy. The attendance in the Upper House at the present day strikingly illustrates the difference between forms and practice.

The 850 hereditary peers are a relic of the feudal Great Council of the middle ages, and their peerages—of England, Scotland, Ireland, Great Britain or the United Kingdom—reflect the historical relations between the various parts of the Kingdom. The presence of the 25 Lords Spiritual is a reminder, both that the medieval prelates attended as great landowners and of the continuing establishment of the Church of England. The nine statutory Lords of Appeal in Ordinary carry on in a professional way the ancient jurisdiction of the High Court of Parliament as the final court of appeal from most courts in the land. Although it is anomalous that judges should sit in the Legislature, it is convenient that the Lords of Appeal and a few other senior judges who have peerages should assist the deliberations of the House in that way. Mr. Wilson's reconstructed Ministry included eleven members of the House of Lords, two of them members of the Cabinet—the Lord Chancellor and the Lord President of the Council who was also Leader of the House.

Most anomalous of all is the Lord Chancellor, the holder of what is probably the oldest office in the country after the Crown—at least, he counts St. Swithin among his predecessors. He performs important functions of a legislative, executive and judicial nature.

Although Speaker of the House of Lords he speaks and votes as a politician, and he has not the powers of the Speaker of the Commons for maintaining order in the House and giving rulings. The Lord Chancellor is a Minister of the Crown, almost invariably a member of the Cabinet, and the principal legal and constitutional adviser of the Government. He is also head of the Judiciary, presiding over the House of Lords when sitting in its judicial capacity and the Judicial Committee of the Privy Council. He also recommends the appointment of Judges of the High Court and County Courts; appoints and removes Recorders, Stipendiary Magistrates and Justices of the Peace in England, and various other judicial or quasi-judicial officers; accepts a continuing responsibility for law reform; controls the Land Registry, the Public Trustee Office and Court records; and he is the patron of some hundreds of Anglican benefices. This multifarious work is done with the help of a small office staff. So long as we have highly competent and extremely hard-working Lord Chancellors, the system works and can work well; but the time must surely not be far off when the range and complexity of the duties become too much for one man–perhaps if the responsibility for the staff and buildings of all Courts is added, as recommended by the Royal Commission on Assizes and Quarter Sessions. He could be assisted by a Vice-Chancellor, though the revived title might now be misleading. Otherwise the non-judicial functions would have to be given to a Minister of Justice.

RECENT REFORMS

Five piecemeal reforms to the House of Lords have been made in recent years. First, peers have been allowed expenses of attendance, 3 guineas a day from 1957 and now £6-10s. a day, plus travelling expenses. Secondly, the Life Peerages Act 1958 empowered the Crown to create peers and peeresses for life with the right to sit and vote in the House of Lords. The object was to increase the number of persons (especially non-Conservatives) with both the time and the inclination to attend and to speak regularly. It was the intention that the Prime Minister should consult the Leader of the Opposition and accept his suggestions. Thirdly, at the time of the passing of the Life Peerages Act, Standing Orders were amended so that Lords could apply for leave of absence for a session or the remainder of the Parliament. A Lord who has been granted leave of absence is expected not to attend until the period has expired, but the House has no power to exclude members. About 200 peers apply for leave of absence. By ancient custom peers have a duty to attend, though the House no longer enforces attendance and fewer hereditary peers come to perform their duty. Fourthly, the Peerage Act 1963 permitted the disclaimer of hereditary peerages, generally within one year of succession, and advantage was taken of this by such actual or would-be Prime Ministers as Sir Alec Douglas-Home, Mr. Quintin Hogg and Mr. Wedgwood Benn. Disclaimer of a hereditary peerage ought logically to bar the heirs, but the Act effected the unsatisfactory compromise of making a disclaimer operate for life only. Lastly, women have been admitted to the House of Lords (which thereby becomes a misnomer), life peeresses by the Act of 1958 and hereditary peeresses by the Act of 1963.

The 1,062 members of the House of Lords on 1 August 1968 were composed of: 858 hereditary peers (736 by succession and 122 of first creation); 155 life peers (over 100 of whom were created by Mr. Wilson); 23 serving or retired Law Lords and 26 Bishops. Fewer than 300 attended more than one-third of the sittings of the House or its Committees in the session 1967–68, but the average daily attendance was then about 230 compared with 92 in 1955. Of those who attended more than one-third of the sittings in 1967–68 about 125 took the Conservative whip, about 95 took the Labour whip, about 20 took the Liberal whip and about 50 were cross-benchers, so that Conservatives had ceased to form a majority of those who attend most regularly. It is a convention that the 'Law Lords' (Lords of Appeal and other judges who may hold peerages, such as the Lord Chief Justice) do not take part in political controversy, a convention broken by Lord Carson over the Anglo-Irish Treaty in 1922. They make valuable contributions in technical questions of law.

84

PARLIAMENT: THE SECOND CHAMBER

The functions and powers of the House of Lords have been reviewed from time to time during the present century. From the Bryce Report (1918), the Conference of Party Leaders (1948) and the recent White Paper on House of Lords Reform (1968), we may summarise and comment on the generally accepted conclusions as follows:

(1) The provision of a forum for full and free debate on general matters of public interest, especially important questions unconnected with specific legislative proposals for which the House of Commons cannot find the time, for example, foreign policy, the economic situation, defence and Commonwealth affairs. The House of Lords is now the only Parliamentary vehicle for the expression of independent opinion.

(2) The revision of Public Bills brought from the House of Commons, which has more limited time for discussion. 'Revision' here amounts to the proposal of amendments. Debate is mainly on the Committee stage, which is held on the floor of the House. In communications with the other House concerning amendments, written messages have replaced the former conferences, though there are also sometimes informal discussions between party leaders. The Second Chamber provides an opportunity for Government Bills to be 'cleared up' by drafting amendments, amendments consequential to those made in the House of Commons and amendments designed to meet criticisms in the Commons. Such amendments are mostly proposed by the Government itself. In the session 1946–47 1200 amendments were proposed in the House of Lords, of which 95 per cent were accepted by the Commons, though the number of Lords' amendments in recent years has been considerably less. Peers sometimes propose valuable changes, but in the case of Government Bills they would seldom insist on their amendments. Disorder and obstruction are unknown. Speeches are more concise than in the Commons, and late sittings are very rare.

(3) The initiation of Bills, especially Government Bills of a

politically less controversial nature and Private Members' Bills. Not many of the latter are introduced into the Upper House nowadays. Government Bills introduced there have included such topics as Crown Proceedings, Commonwealth Constitutions and Independence Acts, Judicature, copyright and forestry. It is desirable that a fair proportion of Government Bills should be introduced into the Second Chamber, otherwise it would have too little legislative work at the beginning of the session and too much towards the end.

(4) The consideration of subordinate legislation.

(5) The consideration of Private Bills, which is mostly done in small Select Committees.

(6) The scrutiny of the activities of the Government.

As the White Paper on House of Lords Reform pointed out, all these functions have to be performed by Parliament, and in recent years the House of Lords has got through more work and made an increasing contribution. It relieves the Commons of much of the dull but arduous task of examining Private Bills and subordinate legislation. Since the judicial business of the House is now done by an Appellate Committee, the House is able to meet at 2.30 p.m., instead of having to wait (as formerly) until 4 p.m.

POWERS OF THE HOUSE OF LORDS

With regard to powers, the results of House of Lords debates do not affect the fate of Governments. A common practice is to 'move for papers', but after discussion the motion is usually withdrawn instead of the House proceeding to vote.

The Lords have no powers over finance. Since the Restoration the Commons have denied the right of the Lords to introduce or to amend Money Bills as defined in Standing Orders: the grant of supply and taxation are entirely within the discretion of the Commons. The Finance Bill is usually the subject of a short debate on the second reading in the Lords, without a division, whether or not it is certified as a Money Bill for the purposes of the Parliament Act 1911.

The House of Lords has the legal power to refuse its consent to

Bills, but the effect of the Parliament Acts is to turn the power of rejection into a power of delay. The purpose of the delaying power according to the Bryce Report is to enable the opinion of the nation to be adequately expressed, especially on Bills affecting the fundamentals of the Constitution, or introducing new principles of legislation, or raising issues on which the opinion of the country appears to be equally divided. At the Conference of Party Leaders in 1948 the Conservatives also thought a limited delaying power necessary to enable the electorate to be properly informed and public opinion to express itself; but the Labour spokesmen contended that its purpose was to enable the House of Commons (who must be regarded as the interpreters of public opinion) to think again. Tied up with this question of principle is the question, what is a 'reasonable' period of delay?

TWO HOUSES IN CONFLICT: THE PARLIAMENT ACT 1911

The Parliament Act 1911 was introduced by a Liberal Government as a result of the rejection by the Lords of a number of the Government's measures, notably the Finance Bill of 1909 containing Lloyd George's Budget. The preamble recites that it was intended to substitute for the existing House of Lords a second chamber constituted on a popular instead of an hereditary basis, but such substitution could not be immediately brought into operation; that provision would require thereafter to be made for limiting and defining the powers of the new second chamber, but that it was expedient meanwhile to make provision restricting the existing powers of the House of Lords. And so this fundamental constitutional statute was opportunist in inception and temporary in intention. It was passed by the House of Lords with the help of many abstentions induced by the threat that they would be swamped by the creation of hundreds of new peerages.

The provisions of the Parliament Act 1911 with regard to 'Money Bills', that is, Bills dealing *only* with taxation, supply, appropriation and certain other specified matters, remain in force. Indeed the power of the House of Lords in relation thereto could hardly be diminished, as in effect peers have not less than one month in which to look at them, and then (unless the Commons direct to the contrary, which they are not likely to do) they become law on receiving the Royal assent, whether the Lords have consented to them (as they always now do) or not. The Speaker's certificate that a Bill is a Money Bill as defined in the Act 'shall be conclusive for all purposes', which expression would cover the Lords and the Sovereign, and 'shall not be questioned in any Court of law'. We may ask whether one person, even the holder of an office with the traditions of the Speaker's, should be entrusted with the extraordinary power of issuing a conclusive certificate of this kind. The only sanction against its abuse would be impeachment, and the Select Committee on Parliamentary Privilege has recommended that impeachment be abolished. Sir Ivor Jennings suggested that the certificate should be given either by a Judge or by a Joint Committee. It is true that the Act directs the Speaker to consult 'if practicable' two members from the Chairmen's Panel, but a Joint Committee of both Houses seems preferable, and in fact such a Committee presided over by the Speaker was proposed by the Government in 1922 and again in 1927.

With regard to other Public Bills (except Bills to extend the maximum duration of Parliament, which are discussed later), the Parliament Act 1911, as amended by the 'Act' of 1949, provides that such Bills may be presented for the Royal assent and become law without the consent of the Lords, if they have been passed by the Commons in two (amended from three) successive sessions, whether of the same Parliament or not, and rejected by the Lords on each occasion, provided that one year (amended from two years) has elapsed since the first second reading in the Commons. There is not much in the requirement of two (previously three) sessions, as the Government can arrange a prorogation after a very short session and can apply the Guillotine. The Speaker's certificate that these requirements have been complied with is, again, 'conclusive for all purposes, and shall not be questioned in any Court of law'.

Alternatives to a period of delay suggested in the debate on the 1911 Bill were that acute controversial differences should be decided by referendum, or (as to less serious matters) by a joint sitting of both Houses with the Speaker as chairman. Other Lords' amendments would have excluded certain fundamental or constitutional matters from the operation of the Bill. The method of settling differences suggested by the Bryce Committee was a free conference of thirty members from each House, sitting in secret.

The power of rejection is unfettered in relation to Bills to extend the maximum duration of Parliament beyond five years. Thus the House of Lords remains the only safeguard (if refusal of the Royal assent is regarded as obsolete) against extensions of the life of Parliament at the will of the Commons alone. The exclusion from section 2 of the Parliament Act 1911 of Bills to extend the maximum life of Parliament cannot itself be said to be capable of being repealed or amended (whether expressly or impliedly) under the special provisions of that Act by employing the argument from the 'sovereignty' or legally unlimited legislative power of Parliament, because the Parliament that is 'sovereign' consists of the Queen, Lords and Commons, whereas a measure passed under the provisions of the Parliament Act would be passed by the Queen and Commons only.

The provisional nature of the Parliament Act 1911 is shown by its failure to cover such matters as Finance and other Supply Bills not certified as Money Bills; Bills to confirm Provisional Orders; Government Bills introduced into the House of Lords; Statutory Instruments; and delaying tactics until prorogation puts an end to the session, thus postponing the operation of the Act until yet another session. The rejection by the Lords of a statutory Order relating to United Nations sanctions against Rhodesia in 1968 drew attention to the topic of delegated legislation, though the Lords did not maintain their opposition to an equivalent Order subsequently introduced.

Owing to the restraint shown by the Lords and the fact that the period was dominated by Conservative Governments, only two Acts were passed before 1949 without the consent of the House of Lords, namely, the Government of Ireland Act 1914 (which never in fact came into force) and the Welsh Church Act 1914. The

Lords have occasionally rejected Bills in circumstances that did not lead to the adoption of the Parliament Act procedure, either because a compromise was reached or because the Bill was dropped on account of war or a general election. Examples are the Temperance (Scotland) Bill 1912–13 and the Rabbits Bill 1928.

There is no reason in principle why the Lords should not reject a Private Member's Bill sent up from the Commons. If they do, it is not likely that the Parliament Act procedure could be complied with in the next session unless the Government adopt the Bill. Sydney Silverman introduced into the Labour Government's Criminal Justice Bill of 1948 an amendment to abolish the death penalty, which was carried on a free vote against the advice of the Home Secretary. The House of Lords rejected this clause. The Home Secretary proposed a compromise in the Commons which was rejected by the Lords, and the Government then dropped the clause as otherwise the whole Bill would have lapsed at the end of the session. In 1956 the Conservative Government allowed time in the Commons for a Private Member's Bill to abolish the death penalty: the Bill was passed against the advice of the Home Secretary, but was rejected by the Lords. At that time the Lords probably represented public opinion.

THE 'PARLIAMENT ACT 1949'

The 'Parliament Act 1949' is in form an amendment to the Parliament Act 1911, designed to reduce the period of the Lords' delaying power over Public Bills other than Money Bills from two years to one year, spread over two sessions instead of three. This also was an occasional measure, devised to meet a particular crisis. The Labour Government, having come to the end of a series of nationalisation Bills for which it had a mandate at the previous general election, wanted to proceed to nationalise the iron and steel industry, a policy strongly opposed by the directors of the industry but not one which aroused much interest in the general public. The stage had been reached when, if the House of Lords rejected the proposed Iron and Steel Bill, there would not be time to get it through in the lifetime of the existing Parliament by using the procedure of the Parliament Act 1911. So in 1947 the Government introduced a Parliament Bill which the Conservative majority in the Lords opposed on the grounds that it did not reform the Upper House, the nation had expressed no desire for it, and it would go far to expose the country to the dangers of single chamber government. The Bill was retrospective in that it extended to cover any Bill that might have been rejected a second time by the House of Lords before the Royal assent was given to the Parliament Bill itself. A Conference of Party Leaders, as has been mentioned, broke down after failing to reach agreement over the delaying power. The Lords then rejected the Parliament Bill, which eventually received the Royal assent in 1949 *without the consent of the House of Lords* under the provisions of the Parliament Act 1911, an extra short session being introduced for the purpose. Incidentally, the Iron and Steel Act was not forced through under these retroactive provisions for, although the Lords insisted on their amendment to postpone the vesting date until after the general election, the Government accepted the principle by inserting a provision that the Iron and Steel Corporation should not be appointed before a date that would be after the election, which in fact the Government lost. The limitation of the power of the House of Lords has been said to have benefited the Executive rather than the House of Commons.

IS THE 'PARLIAMENT ACT 1949' A VALID ACT?

We have already thrown doubt in chapter 1 on the validity of the 'Parliament Act 1949' as an Act of Parliament. We are not arguing–as it is impossible in English law to argue–that an Act of Parliament is invalid. What we are questioning is whether the measure calling itself 'the Parliament Act 1949' bears the character of an Act of Parliament. Coke's report of *The Prince's Case* (1606) says that it is no Act if it be stated to have been passed by the King with the assent of one House only. This statement must now be read subject to the Parliament Act 1911, *passed with the consent of the House of Lords*, in accordance with the provisions of which–as we have seen–Bills (with certain exceptions) may be certified to have been passed by the Queen by and with the consent of the Commons. The Lords retained after 1911 any power they had at common law that was not expressly abrogated by the Parliament Act of that year. Now it is a general principle, both of law and logic, that a person or body on whom powers are conferred cannot assume greater powers than are granted. The Parliament Act 1911 did not confer on the House of Lords a power to delay the passage of Bills: it restricted the common law power of that House to reject Bills. What the Parliament Act 1911 may be said to have done is to have delegated law-making power to the Queen and the Commons under certain specific conditions, and it is not open to them as delegates to enlarge that power. In other words, the Parliament Act 1911, as the parent or enabling Act, cannot itself be amended by subordinate legislation of the Queen and the Commons.

This argument concerning legislation to reduce the period of delay may probably be extended to legislation affecting the existence of the House of Lords, and perhaps also its composition. The continued existence of the House of Lords in some form is certainly implied by the Parliament Act 1911.

At the time of writing no Act has purported to be passed without the consent of the Lords 'in accordance with the provisions of the Parliament Acts 1911 and 1949', so no legislation yet stands in jeopardy as depending on the doubtful effectiveness of the 'Act' of 1949.

Whenever the Lords show signs of rejecting or insisting on amendments to a Government Bill sent up from the Commons, some exasperated Minister or member in the Commons utters the threat that the procedure of the Parliament Acts will or should be employed to diminish the delaying power still further, or to abolish the House of Lords altogether. From what we have said above, it may be doubted whether either of these threats could lawfully be carried out.

The swamping of the Upper House by the creation of a sufficient number of peers to ensure the passage of a Bill is, in Balfour's words, 'not a remedy but a revolution'. The threat to do so—even if they were now to be life peers – would not only be contrary to the spirit of the Parliament Act 1911, and perhaps contrary to convention, but would be unworthy of a country claiming to have a rational system of government.

The 'conclusiveness' of the Speaker's certificate that the provisions of the Parliament Acts have been complied with, need not be accepted as a cloak for what would appear on the face of them to be invalid amendments of the 1911 Act. There is high judicial authority for saying that where a statute states that an instrument, such as an order or certificate, shall be 'conclusive evidence' or words to that effect, this implies that the instrument has been properly made, and does not extend to some purported order or certificate which was beyond the power of the maker to make. One of the latest instances is *Anisminic* v. *Foreign Compensation Commission* (1969), where the House of Lords held that the provision in the Foreign Compensation Act 1950 that the determination by the Foreign Compensation Commission of any application made to them under the Act should not be called in question in any court of law, ought not to be interpreted as including everything that purported to be a 'determination' but was not in fact one because the Commission had misconstrued the Order in which its jurisdiction was defined. The same argument could be applied to a certificate signed by the Speaker in misconstruction of the power conferred on him by the Parliament Act 1911.

The abolition of the House of Lords by a simple one-clause Bill, so dear to the hearts of iconoclasts, is not practicable anyway, because some provision would have to be made for the existing functions of the House of Lords, apart from that of general debate. If there were no revising body, the procedure of the House of Commons would require alteration. The law relating to Private Bills and certain kinds of subordinate legislation would have to be amended, and the duties of the Commons in these matters would be greatly increased. Modifications would have to be made in the law relating to elections and seats in the House of Commons. Also, arrangements would need to be made concerning the judicial functions of the House of Lords, and the method of removing judges would have to be changed.

WHEN WILL THE LORDS STICK IT OUT?

Lord Salisbury suggested in the debate on the War Damage Bill 1965 that the Lords should only insist on their amendments if: (1) the question raises issues important enough to justify such drastic action; and (2) the issue is one that can be readily understood by the people and on which the Lords can expect their support, an issue on which the House of Lords would really be acting as the watchdog of the people. His advice was enough to persuade the Lords on that occasion not to insist on their amendment which, by omitting the *ex post facto* provision, would have frustrated the main purpose of the Bill, which was to nullify the decision of the House of Lords in the *Burmah Oil Company Case*.

In 1969 the Opposition in the Upper House decided not to oppose the Redistribution of Seats (No. 2) Bill on second reading, but to move a number of amendments in Committee, the effect of which would be to implement the recommendations of the Boundary Commission with regard to the provinces. Government supporters in both Houses condemned this action as interference with the composition of the House of Commons, a matter which concerned that House alone. Opposition peers, on the other hand, regarded the Bill as gerrymandering and therefore as unconstitutional practice which it was duty of a Second Chamber to prevent. The 'wrecking' amendments were passed by 270 votes to 96, a majority of 174, the Conservatives being supported by Liberal and cross-bench peers. Analysis of the voting shows that the Government would still have been defeated even if hereditary peers had not voted. The Lords also rejected a revised version of the Bill by 229—78 votes, a majority of 151. Although their action was in defence of a constitutional principle it can scarcely be regarded as a 'classic' case because the Bill concerned representation in the House of Commons.

PARLIAMENT: THE SECOND CHAMBER

Most countries have, in addition to their representative Assembly, a Second Chamber, Upper House or Senate, elected indirectly or by some different method from the Assembly, or nominated in some way. Hamilton in *The Federalist* warned of the danger of accumulating in a single body all the most important prerogatives of sovereignty, and thus entailing on posterity 'one of the most execrable forms of government that human infatuation ever contrived'. In a federation or confederation a Second Chamber is regarded as essential in order to preserve the arrangements for the distribution of powers and the rights of the constituent units. In a unitary State, where these considerations do not apply, a Second Chamber is still generally thought desirable for all or some of the following reasons:

(1) To act as a break on important constitutional changes, such as prolonging the life of the elected Chamber, interfering with the independence of the Judiciary, tampering with the institutions of government (such as free and fair elections), and restricting the rights of individuals.

(2) To impose a period of delay, to give time for second thoughts, and generally to act as a check on hasty and ill-considered legislation.

(3) To represent distinct interests in the community.

(4) To facilitate the presence in the Legislature of persons with special experience or qualifications, who are not likely to stand for election or to be elected if they stand.

(5) To revise, or suggest amendments to, Bills sent up from the other Chamber.

(6) To relieve members of the Lower House from much, or at least some, of their committee work.

(7) To debate matters of general policy, such as foreign affairs and defence, in a relatively independent atmosphere.

(8) To introduce Bills that are not politically controversial.

(9) To relieve the Lower House from much of the work of considering Private Bills.

In relation to this country the vital matter is item (1). These are changes which, with a written Constitution, would require a Constitutional Amendment. Then, if there is to be further devolution to Scotland and Wales and the Islands, and perhaps the regions of England, it might be thought desirable that these areas should be in some way specially represented in the Second Chamber. The other items listed above are also important in varying degrees.

Although it is an illusion to suppose that any Second Chamber can be completely non-political, at least it can be less partisan than the Lower House. Sir Dingle Foot entered a plea for the retention of a Second Chamber in a letter to *The Times* of January 13, 1967, in which he wrote: 'To abolish the Second Chamber would give the Executive increased immunity from Parliamentary supervision and enhance the authority of the Party machines'. The delaying power, in his view, should not be eliminated: our electoral system does not ensure that the majority in the House of Commons necessarily represents the majority of the electors, and there is still therefore a case for the Lords being able to require the Commons to have second thoughts within, say, six months. Even Mr. Crossman has become a convert to bicameralism, as he confessed when introducing the White Paper on House of Lords Reform into the Commons in 1968. But when we have reformed the Upper House to the general satisfaction, much of the benefit will be lost unless the composition and powers of the reformed Upper House are entrenched against future tinkering by temporary majorities in the Commons. This can only be done, as will be argued in the last chapter, if we adopt a written Constitution with judicial review.

PROPOSALS FOR REFORM: POWERS

A reformed Upper House must retain some power of delay, or even rejection, if we are to be preserved from single chamber government; if it is to exercise any influence in public affairs, and its expressions of opinion are to be taken seriously by the Commons and the public; and if it is to be a body to which suitable persons would be willing to belong. The period of delay should preferably not be shorter than that provided in the Parliament Act 1911. The power of rejection must continue to apply to Bills to prolong the life of Parliament, and should perhaps extend to Bills affecting the composition or powers of the Second Chamber. Professor Bernard Crick would take away the delaying power altogether, and impose on the new Upper House a load of detailed fact-finding Committee work on behalf of the House of Commons. His Second Chamber would be little more than the Prime Minister's devil. Who would want to sit in a kennel of toothless dogs-bodies?

The Government White Paper and the Parliament (No. 2) Bill of 1968 were more realistic than this, being based on the results of an informal conference of party leaders from both Houses, as agreed up to the time when the Prime Minister broke off the discussions because the Lords rejected a statutory instrument. With regard to a Public Bill sent up by the House of Commons—other than a Money Bill, a Bill to extend the maximum duration of Parliament or a Bill to confirm a provisional order—the Parliament Bill would have fixed the period of delay as six months from the day on which the House of Lords disagreed a Bill of this sort; and a resolution of the Commons to present such Bills for the Royal assent without the Lords' consent would not be affected by prorogation or dissolution. In case the Lords postponed an overt disagreement, the Commons would be empowered to resolve that the Bill be treated as having been disagreed by the Lords. The Parliament Bill also included provisions to the effect that resolutions of the House of Lords concerning the making, coming into operation or continuance in force of subordinate legislation could be overridden by the House of Commons. Sections 2 and 5 of the Parliament Act 1911 and the whole of the 'Parliament Act 1949' would be repealed.

PROPOSALS FOR REFORM: COMPOSITION

The logical order in which it is generally considered that the problems of a Second Chamber should be dealt with is, first,

97

functions and powers; and secondly, composition. The main objection taken to the composition of the House of Lords is the hereditary element, which involves not only the right to sit and vote on the part of persons who may be quite unsuitable, but also the prospect of armies of 'backwoodsmen' turning up suddenly to vote in an important division. It is also largely due to the hereditary element that the Upper House in recent times has been predominantly Conservative, though this factor has been modified by the effects of the Life Peerages Act 1958. On the other hand, the House of Lords benefits from the advice of the occasional expert and the wide age spread of hereditary peers, and the backwoodsmen do not obstruct.

The well-qualified and objective Bryce Conference considered five alternative methods of composition in order to secure the predominance of the popular element in the Upper House, namely: (a) nomination, (b) direct election by large constituencies, (c) election on a regional basis by groups of local authorities, (d) selection by a joint standing committee of both Houses, and (e) election by the House of Commons. They recommended that the Second Chamber should consist (in addition to the Lord Chancellor and Law Lords) of: (1) 246 persons elected by panels of members of the House of Commons distributed in certain territorial areas, the period of tenure to be twelve years, one-third to retire every four years; and (2) 81 persons elected by a joint standing committee of both Houses, to hold office and to retire in the same way as the first group. These proposals were not taken up at the time, partly because there was disagreement among the members of the Bryce Conference themselves.

A Functional or Vocational Chamber is mooted from time to time, either as a Second or possibly a Third Chamber. The idea is that the Lower House represents people geographically, and the Upper House (or one of the Upper Houses) should represent them in relation to their various professions and occupations. Some form of electoral colleges would have to be devised. Experience in other countries shows that a Functional or Vocational Chamber may have a limited use in an advisory capacity, but that as part of a Legislature it will in time be so manipulated that it will become as much a party Chamber as the Lower House.

The Conference of Party Leaders that met in 1948, which we have already mentioned, agreed that the following proposals for the reform of the Upper House should be further considered if agreement could be reached on the extent of the delaying power:

'(1) The Second Chamber should be complementary to and not a rival to the Lower House, and, with this end in view, the reform of the House of Lords should be based on a modification of its existing constitution as opposed to the establishment of a Second Chamber of a completely new type based on some system of election.

(2) The revised constitution of the House of Lords should be such as to secure as far as practicable that a permanent majority is not assured for any one political Party.

(3) The present right to attend and vote based solely on heredity should not by itself constitute a qualification for admission to a reformed Second Chamber.

(4) Members of the Second Chamber should be styled 'Lords of Parliament' and would be appointed on grounds of personal distinction or public service. They might be drawn either from Hereditary Peers, or from commoners who would be created Life Peers.

(5) Women should be capable of being appointed Lords (*sic*) of Parliament in like manner as men.

(6) Provision should be made for the inclusion in the Second Chamber of certain descendants of the Sovereign, certain Lords Spiritual and the Law Lords.

(7) In order that persons without private means should not be excluded, some remuneration would be payable to members of the Second Chamber.

(8) Peers who were not Lords of Parliament should be entitled to stand for election to the House of Commons, and also to vote at elections in the same manner as other citizens.

(9) Some provision should be made for the disqualification of a member of the Second Chamber who neglects, or becomes no

longer able or fitted, to perform his duties as such' (Cmnd. 7380, §3).

An interesting suggestion made before the passing of the Life Peerages Act was put forward by Mr. Anthony Wedgwood Benn in 1957, that the Second Chamber should be composed of those members of the Privy Council who do not sit in the House of Commons. At that time this would have produced an Upper House composed of 206 Privy Councillors, of whom 125 would be peers (93 of the first creation) and 81 commoners other than M.P.'s. Of the peers concerned fewer than half were Conservatives, one-sixth were Labour and nearly one-third were non-party. This would provide a new Second Chamber ready-made, even though the average age would be rather high, and one advantage of the hereditary system is that it creates opportunities for younger men. A considerable overlap was found between the Privy Council and peers who were active in the House of Lords. Mr. Benn judged the quality of Privy Councillors as higher than the quality of peers, traced a strong historical case for the change, and pointed out that it would enable the Judicial Committee to continue the appellate work of the House of Lords. Mr. Benn was not clear whether a Privy Councillor in the House of Commons would have a right to apply for a writ of attendance to the House of Lords, and (if so) whether he would for ever after be disqualified from being elected to the House of Commons. The main weakness of Mr. Benn's scheme is that it made no provision for the future: the new House of Lords would depend for its continuance on unfettered nomination by the Prime Minister.

THE PARLIAMENT BILL 1968

The Parliament (No. 2) Bill 1968 was an ingenious attempt to devise a reformed Second Chamber that would avoid what are generally agreed to be the defects in the composition of the present Chamber, that would provide the kind of Second Chamber considered suitable, and would at the same time preserve as far as practicable the historical continuity of the House of Lords without interfering with hereditary titles. Direct election was properly turned down on the ground that a directly elected Second Chamber would be a rival to the House of Commons and could claim at least equal powers with it, and would also violate our Parliamentary system whereby the Government is responsible to the Commons.

Not much was said about indirect election. A regional basis for indirect election or nomination was thought to be premature. Appropriate institutions in Scotland, Wales, Northern Ireland and the regions of England do not at present exist, and the organisation of local government in Britain is in the melting pot. Also it was feared that rivalry might develop between a regionally-constituted Second Chamber and the House of Commons. Yet indirect election on a regional basis might well be the most satisfactory method.

A Second Chamber composed entirely of members nominated for the duration of one Parliament was also rejected, as it would merely reflect the political complexion of the House of Commons, as well as unduly increasing the Government's power of patronage. Little was said about nomination for fixed and staggered terms of years, a method which, either alone or as a supplement to Life Peers, enjoys wide support.

The solution adopted in the Bill was a two-tier scheme of voting and other (non-voting) members of the House of Lords, an idea that goes back at least to 1948. Voting peers would be peers of first creation, that is, life peers and the first holders of hereditary peerages, who have made a declaration that they wish to take advantage of this qualification. They would lose their voting right on reaching the age of 72, or by failing to attend one-third of the meetings in a session otherwise than through sick-leave or leave of absence. The voting peers would number about 230. The non-voting members of the House would be those peers by succession who had already received or applied for a writ of summons before the commencement of the Act, though any of these could disclaim membership of the House within one year. Non-voting members would retain their right to move any motion and to take part (otherwise than by vote) in any proceedings of the

House or any committee. Attendance regulations would be modified for Ministers, Lords of Appeal and the Lords Spiritual. These last would be gradually reduced in number from 26 to 16. The Bill did not mention denominations other than the Church of England.

The Bill further provided that all Lords Spiritual and Temporal could vote at Parliamentary elections, and that a peer who was not entitled to sit in the House of Lords should not be disqualified from sitting in the House of Commons.

The party complexion of a reformed House of Lords raises difficult problems. Two apparently conflicting principles were emphasised in the White Paper. One was that an effective Second Chamber must possess a degree of genuine independence, and the other was that the Government of the day must be able to expect that its measures, though subject to scrutiny, would normally be passed without undue delay. The solution adopted was that the Government should have a majority of (say) 10 per cent of the *party* membership, but not a majority over all members including the cross-benchers who form such a valuable independent element. Creation of new peers (who would presumably be life peers) would continue to be done under the prerogative, that is, on the nomination of the Prime Minister; and the preamble to the Bill referred to the policy set out in the White Paper, namely, (*a*) to preserve among the voting members of the reformed House of Lords a proper balance between members of the Government party, members of other parties and members of no party; and (*b*) to include a suitable number of voting peers with knowledge of and experience in matters of special concern to the various countries, nations and regions of the United Kingdom. The White Paper did not mention the provision in the Act of Union that Scotland should be represented in the House of Lords by not fewer than 16 peers of Scotland. The Prime Minister is expected to consult the leaders of other parties over the choice (though not the number) of new peers belonging to their parties. The idea is that the incoming Government would achieve its majority of roughly 10 per cent over the other parties by means of a suitable number of new creations during its first months of office. The balance of power would in theory be held by the cross-benchers, but it is said that in practice they do not at present possess any corporate sense or act as an organised group.

All is left, then, to the discretion of the Prime Minister of the day. The White Paper suggested–though this was not in the Bill–that there might be a Committee (appointed and dismissible by whom?) to review periodically the composition of the reformed Upper House and to report, either to the Prime Minister or to Parliament, on any deficiencies in the balance and range of the membership of the House. It seems to be implied that the reviewing Committee would consider the balance in relation to the state of the parties in the House of Commons, which could freeze the position at the last general election as modified by chance by-elections. A weak or unpopular Government would be fortified by its working majority in the Upper House, for there is no suggestion that the reviewing Committee would look periodically at the public opinion polls. If a Government were normally to have a working majority of this kind in both Houses it would be all the more important, has urged in chapter 3, to shorten the maximum life of Parliament and to hold more frequent general elections. But in any event, the maximum number of the Second Chamber must be fixed, so as to prevent the swamping of the House in order to force through particular measures.

It was the Government's intention that, if the House of Lords were reformed on these lines, the two Houses might function more as a Parliament. The House of Lords could develop a committee system, committees of various kinds might draw their members from both Houses, and a wider range of public Bills might be introduced into the Upper House.

No encouragement was given to a suggestion often heard, that Ministers should be entitled to speak and answer questions (though not to vote) in both Houses. It would have the incidental advantage that any Minister, except the Prime Minister and the Chancellor of the Exchequer, could be a member of the Upper House. The objections are that the status of Ministers within their

Houses would be altered, and that Ministers are already over-burdened with work. The present practice is that every department has a representative in the Commons, and that the Foreign Office and a few other departments should be represented in the Lords.

Strong objection was taken both inside and outside Parliament to the increased patronage that these proposals for the nomination of life peers would give to the Government, the Government party and the Prime Minister. This objection was not allayed by the prospect that the new voting peers would be created for life and not for the duration of a Parliament only, and that the position would be reviewed periodically by some Committee or other. In fact the objection to nomination was all the stronger because the scheme was associated with the payment of full salaries to voting peers. A substantial proportion of indirectly elected members seems to be desirable for the Second Chamber, and some of these could be furnished by representatives of the Nations or Regions if we have a scheme of devolution.

The name of a reformed Second Chamber will need further thought. It is only a minor point that 'Lords' at present includes Ladies. What is more important is that membership of the Upper House must inevitably be separated sooner or later from the hereditary peerage, and therefore there will cease to be much point, if any, in continuing to call members of the Upper House 'peers' or 'Lords'. 'Senate' sounds Roman, American or academic, yet we can hardly return to 'Witenagemot'.

The most significant feature of the Parliament Bill was that it was largely based on proposals agreed by the party leaders of both Houses. From one point of view that is a most desirable state of affairs in dealing with fundamental constitutional changes. And yet there is danger in such an agreement in this instance because the scheme, involving as it does the composition of the Second Chamber by the nomination of life peers, would be of great advantage to each group of party leaders in turn, which is not necessarily the same thing as being of advantage to the nation as a whole. The Bill was violently attacked by the backbenchers on both sides, especially those on the extreme wings, who were suspicious of the dominating position taken up by Ministers and their opposite numbers. The Government, which had previously given way to backbench pressure over the legal sanction clauses in the Prices and Incomes Bill, now extricated itself by dropping the Parliament Bill, ostensibly to allow time for the more urgent Industrial Relations Bill. Thus the influence of backbenchers on the floor of the Commons is far from negligible, though it is unfortunate that it should have led to the shelving of a measure of such far-reaching constitutional importance.

5

The Courts and the Constitution

'The King himself ought not to be subject to man but subject to God and the law', wrote Bracton in the thirteenth century, 'because the law makes him King.' The same view will be found expressed in our medieval law reports, the Year Books of the fourteenth and fifteenth centuries. This superior law governed Kings as well as subjects and set limits to the prerogative. The jurisdiction of the Courts over the prerogative, or common law powers of the Crown, was asserted in such cases as the *Case of Monopolies* (1602) and the *Case of Proclamations* (1610). Most governmental powers are discretionary, as to whether they shall be exercised or how they shall be exercised, or both; but the discretion is limited by the law. What has come to be called 'the rule of law' precludes arbitrary action on the part of the Crown or members of the Government.

The law that is supreme includes statute law as well as common law, and in fact the Government (though not other public authorities) can usually secure the passing by Parliament of such laws as it thinks it needs. So when it was shown in an action brought by Davey Paxman & Co. in 1954 that the Post Office had for many years been charging licence fees for radios in ignorance of the fact that they had no authority to do so, since no regulations with the consent of the Treasury had been issued as required by statute, the Post Office settled the action by repaying the amount of their radio licence and costs. Later in the same year Parliament passed an Act validating the charge for radio licences retrospectively. A Minister or a police constable has powers, common law or statutory, that the ordinary citizen has not; but everyone is *prima facie* equal before the law, and if in proceedings before the

Courts an executive officer claims special powers or immunities, such as apower of arrest or the compulsory purchase of land, he must prove them. In this sense, the Government is subject to law.

The fullest and most valuable elaboration of the 'rule of law' as a supra-national concept was made at a congress of the International Commission of Jurists at Delhi in 1959. In relation to the Executive, the Declaration stated in particular that a citizen who is wronged should have a remedy against the State or Government, and that delegated legislation should be subject to independent judicial control. The English common law was defective with regard to the former, but the Crown Proceedings Act 1947 allowed actions to be brought against Government Departments for breach of contract and tort and in certain other cases where there would be a right of action against private individuals, instead of the citizen having to rely (as previously) on *ex gratia* compensation.

The Declaration of Delhi also related the 'rule of law' to the Judiciary and the legal profession. It requires, in the first place, the independence of the Judiciary, and proper grounds and procedure for the removal of judges. Secondly, it implies an organised and autonomous legal profession on whom a responsibility rests to assist in the maintenance of the rule of law.

The Courts, then, have a vital part to play in controlling the exercise of governmental powers, powers of delegated legislation and powers of adjudication by administrative bodies or tribunals. The Courts have jurisdiction to determine, in an action properly brought before them, whether the purported exercise of a power is authorised by common law or statute. If it is not so authorised, it is *ultra vires* and void. But judicial control goes further than this. As Lord Macnaghten said in *Westminster Corporation* v. *London and North Western Railway* (1905), 'a public body invested with statutory powers ... must take care not to exceed or abuse its powers. It must keep within the limits of the authority committed to it. It must act in good faith. And it must act reasonably.' The question with regard to statutory powers is one of interpretation of the statute concerned. It was held in *Attorney-General* v. *Fulham*

Corporation (1921), for example, that a local authority which had power under a series of Acts to establish baths, wash-houses and open bathing places was not entitled to carry on the business of a laundry, and was acting *ultra vires* in washing customers' clothes as distinct from providing facilities for persons to wash their own clothes. Again, in *White and Collins* v. *Minister of Health* (1939), where a local authority had statutory power to acquire compulsorily for certain purposes any land not forming part of a 'park, garden or pleasure ground', the Court decided that the land concerned did in fact form part of a park, and so set aside a compulsory purchase order that had been confirmed by the Minister.

The methods adopted by the Courts for interpreting or construing statutes have themselves been under scrutiny by legal practitioners and academic lawyers for some time, and this important question is under review by the Law Commission.

A power which is discretionary, that is to say, which is not coupled with a duty to exercise it, is abused or misused if it is exercised for an unauthorised purpose, if relevant considerations are disregarded or irrelevant considerations are taken into account, or if its exercise is grossly unreasonable. Thus it was held in *Hanson* v. *Radcliffe Urban District Council* (1922) that an education authority which had power to dismiss teachers on educational grounds could not dismiss them in order to effect economy; and in *Grice* v. *Dudley Corporation* (1958) a compulsory purchase order made in 1951 in order to provide a car park was set aside as it was based on a notice to treat served in 1939 for the purpose of widening the street and erecting a market hall.

The decision of a public authority can also be upset if it is unreasonable in the sense that the Court considers it to be a decision that no reasonable body could have made. It is not what the Court itself considers unreasonable. Thus the Court of Appeal in *Prescott* v. *Birmingham Corporation* (1955) held that the Birmingham Corporation had no power under either general or local Acts to provide free travel facilities for old people on municipal buses. The Corporation's scheme, said Lord Justice Jenkins, amounted to 'the making of a gift or present in money's worth to a particular section of the local community at the expense of the general body of ratepayers', and in any case it was not a proper exercise of their discretion. Parliament in fact passed an Act later in the same year giving power retrospectively to local authorities to grant established travel concessions to qualified persons. This does not mean that the Court of Appeal was wrong: it means that Parliament had not effectively granted a power which it was widely thought it had granted, and this was an opportunity for the Legislature to be specific where previously it had been vague.

JUDICIAL CONTROL OF DELEGATED LEGISLATION

Judicial control over delegated legislation by means of the *ultra vires* rule is illustrated by the leading case of *Attorney-General* v. *Wilts United Dairies* (1921). The Attorney-General sought to recover £15,000 from Wilts United Dairies, representing a fee of 2d. a gallon on milk purchased by them under licence from the Food Controller, the licence being granted under statutory orders made by virtue of Regulations issued under the Defence of the Realm (Consolidation) Act 1914. The House of Lords decided in favour of Wilts United Dairies on the ground that the charge was a levying of money for the use of the Crown without the authority of Parliament. Neither the Act creating the Ministry of Food, nor the Regulations issued under the Defence of the Realm Act, enabled the Food Controller to levy the payment of any sums of money from any of His Majesty's subjects. In 1925 an Act of Parliament retrospectively validated these charges. Parliament can, of course, expressly delegate the power to levy such charges, and it did so in the last war by the Emergency Powers (Defence) Act 1939. In another leading case arising out of the first world war, *Chester* v. *Bateson* (1920), it was held that a regulation purporting to be made by the Minister of Munitions under the Defence of the Realm Act 1914 was *ultra vires* because it made it an offence to take, without the consent of the Minister, proceedings in the Courts for the recovery of possession of houses occupied by workmen employed on war production in special areas, so long as they continued to pay rent and to observe the other conditions of the tenancy. The landlord might wish to question whether the tenant was a workman so employed, or he might be mistaken either in law or fact as to whether the tenant had paid his rent or violated some other condition of his tenancy. Reasonable conditions for the taking of such proceedings might have been valid, but the Act gave the Minister no power to prohibit under penalty the taking of any judicial proceedings without his consent.

Again, in *Commissioners of Customs and Excise* v. *Cure and Deeley* (1962) a purchase tax regulation which provided that if any person furnished an incomplete return the Commissioners might determine the amount of tax appearing to them to be due and demand payment thereof, which amount should be deemed to be the proper tax due unless it was shown within seven days *to the satisfaction of the Commissioners* that some other amount was due, was held *ultra vires* the Finance (No. 2) Act 1940. It is worth noticing that a Purchase Tax Act in the following year provided that where a person does not keep proper accounts and the Commissioners estimate the amount of tax due, this amount shall be recoverable *unless in any action relating thereto* the person liable proves that a less amount is due.

JUDICIAL CONTROL OF ADMINISTRATIVE JURISDICTION

Judicial control of administrative jurisdiction involves the application of the principles of 'natural justice' evolved by the Courts. There is authority for regarding the requirements of natural justice as part of the *ultra vires* rule, since neither statute nor common law confers jurisdiction to make decisions adversely affecting the rights of individuals in disregard of those principles.

The first and most fundamental principle of natural justice is that a person should not be judge in his own cause. This principle is not confined to administrative tribunals: most of the cases have concerned the ordinary Courts, especially Justices of the Peace whether exercising their criminal or their licensing jurisdiction. Indeed, the leading case concerned the Lord Chancellor himself. In *Dimes* v. *Grand Junction Canal* (1852) the House of Lords set aside a decree made in the Court of Chancery by Lord Chancellor

Cottenham, who unknown to the defendant had an interest as a shareholder in the plaintiff Company, granting an injunction to the Company and confirming their title to certain land it had bought for the purpose of making a canal. It was not suggested that Lord Cottenham was influenced by the interest he had in the canal company, but any person or body exercising powers of a judicial nature must avoid even the appearance of acting under a personal interest.

The other main principle of natural justice is expressed in the maxim, '*audi alteram partem*' (hear the other party). This means that each party must have reasonable notice of the case he has to meet: he must be given an opportunity to state his case, and to answer any arguments put forward by the other side. In criminal law the maxim takes the form: 'no one ought to be condemned unheard'. Again, many of the earlier cases concerned summary proceedings before Justices of the Peace, but during the past century there have been many cases affecting housing, public health and planning authorities. The principle '*audi alteram partem*' in the non-criminal cases to which it applies does not necessarily mean that a person has a right to be heard orally, or that a question must be treated as if it were a trial, nor does it lay down any rules of procedure. As was said in *Board of Education* v. *Rice* (1911) of the duties of the Board of Education in deciding questions arising between local education authorities and school managers: 'they must act in good faith and fairly listen to both sides, for that is the duty lying upon everyone who decides anything'.

There have been decisions and *dicta* in licensing and disciplinary (dismissal) cases that are difficult to reconcile, but they may perhaps in future be brought under the general principle in view of the decision of the House of Lords in *Ridge* v. *Baldwin* (1964). In that case the Chief Constable of Brighton brought an action against the members of the Watch Committee (before the Police Act 1964 came into force) for a declaration that his dismissal for neglect of duty was void. The House of Lords, giving judgment for the Chief Constable, held that the rules of natural justice applied and, as the Watch Committee had not informed him of the charges or given him an opportunity to be heard, except that his solicitor addressed the Committee at one of their two meetings, the Committee's decision was null and void. The Committee ought also to have observed the procedure prescribed by the Police Discipline Regulations issued under the Police Act 1919.

The main need of English administrative law is the simplification of remedies. This is one of the matters covered by the Law Commission's report on Administrative law submitted to the Lord Chancellor in 1969. It has been suggested by one expert, Professor H. W. R. Wade, that we should have what may be called an Administrative Bill of Rights, enacting some of the main principles laid down by the Courts in the field of administrative law, for example, that powers should be exercised reasonably and in good faith, that the principles of natural justice should be presumed to apply unless expressly or impliedly excluded in the enabling Act, and that clauses ousting the jurisdiction of the Courts should not prevent judicial control of excess of jurisdiction. A statute embodying such a Bill of Rights, however, although it might serve the purpose of clarification and uniformity, could be amended or repealed by Parliament at any time and so it would suffer from similar defects to a more general Bill of Rights enacted by the ordinary legislative process, as is argued later in this book.

CROWN PRIVILEGE

Three important exceptions to the general amenability of persons to the law of this country are Parliamentary privilege (which has been discussed in chapter 3), Crown privilege in litigation, and the immunity of Trade Unions in tort.

The Crown Proceedings Act 1947 provided for the first time that in civil proceedings to which the Crown (meaning in effect a Minister or Government Department) is a party, the Crown may be required by the Court to make discovery (i.e. disclosure) of documents, and to produce for inspection any documents relevant to the case; and also that the Crown may be required by the Court to answer interrogatories, or questions put by the other party concerning his case. But a proviso states that this shall be without prejudice to any rule of law which allows the Crown in any case (whether the Crown is a party to the action or not) to withhold any document or to refuse to answer any question on the ground that such disclosure or answer would be injurious to the public interest; and it goes on to preserve the rule that the existence of a document will not be disclosed if, in the opinion of a Minister, it would be injurious to the public interest to disclose its existence. In *Duncan* v. *Cammell, Laird & Co.* (1942), commonly known as the *Thetis Case*, where the common law rules relating to cases where the Crown is not a party were applied, Viscount Simon, Lord Chancellor, said in the House of Lords that where the Crown objected to the production of documents in the public interest, an English Court (as distinct from a Scottish Court or the Judicial Committee of the Privy Council on appeal from overseas) would not inspect the documents concerned. There is no doubt that in the *Thetis Case*–which was a claim for compensation against the builders of a submarine that sank on her trials at the beginning of the last war–the engineers' plans were properly withheld on the ground of national security; but parts of Lord Simon's judgment were *obiter*, and it was not until the House of Lords heard the case of *Conway* v. *Rimmer* in 1968 that the matter could be put on a proper footing. Meanwhile Government departments made claims of privilege that were often excessive and sometimes led to a denial of justice. In *Conway* v. *Rimmer* a former probationary constable wished to bring an action for damages for malicious prosecution against a senior police officer, and asked for the production of certain reports on his probationary period in relation to a minor charge of stealing on which he had been acquitted. The House of Lords held that the Court might call for the documents and decide after inspecting them whether they should be produced. In that case their Lordships examined the reports, found nothing in them the disclosure of which would be in any way prejudicial to the proper administration of the local constabulary or the general public interest, and ordered the defendant to produce the documents for inspection by the plaintiff.

TRADE UNION IMMUNITY

Legislation during the present century concerning trade unions and trade disputes has tended to be *ad hoc*, and on more than one occasion it has been designed to nullify a decision of the House of Lords considered politically undesirable by the Government of the day. Thus section 4 of the Trade Disputes Act 1906 was passed by a Liberal Government, with the support of the infant Labour party, in reaction to the *Taff Vale Case* (1901). This section exempts trade unions from the general law that employers may be sued vicariously for torts committed by their servants or agents in the course of their employment. Moreover, the exemption applies whether or not the tort was committed in furtherance of a trade dispute. Theoretically the legal liability remains but, as the Act provides that no such action against a trade union shall be entertained by any Court, in effect it is an immunity. There is a limited exception in that the trustees of a registered trade union may be sued in any action concerning the property of the union, for example, negligent driving or nuisance, unless it was committed in contemplation or furtherance of a trade dispute. The position with regard to libel or slander is uncertain. It may be added that the individual official is personally liable for the torts he commits, but the purpose of the Act is to preserve trade union funds from the liability to pay damages.

INDEPENDENCE OF THE JUDICIARY FROM THE EXECUTIVE

The famous provisions in the Act of Settlement 1700 that 'Judges' commissions be made *quamdiu se bene gesserint* [during good behaviour], and their salaries ascertained and established, but upon an address of both Houses it may be lawful to remove them', applied to judges of the superior Courts. The first and third of these provisions have been substantially replaced as regards judges of the Supreme Court (except the Lord Chancellor) by the Judicature (Consolidation) Act 1925, and as regards the Lords of Appeal in Ordinary by the Appellate Jurisdiction Act 1876. The second, the ascertainment and establishment of salaries, is secured by the practice–also a convention–of defining judicial salaries in permanent Acts and charging them on the Consolidated Fund. This means that the salaries do not come up for annual review and debate in the Commons, as do most estimates of public expenditure, nor is the Government given an opportunity to bring pressure to bear on judges by threatening to reduce their salaries. These provisions, designed to protect the Judiciary from interference by the Executive, have already been mentioned as one of the most important principles of British constitutional law.

A retiring age of 75 for judges of the superior Courts was introduced by the Judicial Pensions Act 1959. Some Commonwealth Constitutions provide that a judge's salary and conditions of service may not be altered to his detriment during his tenure of office. The Judges' Remuneration Act 1965 provides that judicial salaries may be increased, though not reduced, by Order in Council.

It is commonly stated that judges may be dismissed *only* on an address from both Houses of Parliament; but the meaning of the statutes appears to be that the Crown may dismiss a judge either (*a*) without an address for official misconduct, neglect of official duties, or (probably) conviction for a serious offence; or (*b*) on an address from both Houses for anything that they may regard as misconduct, or perhaps for any reason at all. Such an address must be introduced in the House of Commons, and convention would require the Queen to act upon it. The only removal of a judge following an address since the Act of Settlement was that of an Irish judge in 1830. Abolition of the Upper House, especially one that contains the Law Lords, might be a threat to the independence of the Judiciary, as it would make it easier for the Government to move an address for removal for political motives.

The Act of Settlement was concerned with the security of judicial tenure, not to provide a method for the removal of judges, and the time has come when we ought to consider whether a judicial rather than a Parliamentary process would be more suitable for the latter purpose. We cannot discount the possibility of political bias in the Legislature, especially in the Lower House–it is, after all, a body of politicians, and one could hardly conceive of a less judicial body to decide the question of the removal of a judge. Some of the older Commonwealth Constitutions follow the English law on this matter. Some provide that judges may *only* be removed by the Crown on an address from both Houses (or the House) of the Legislature. Some require 'proved' or 'stated' misbehaviour or incapacity; others specify a minimum majority in one or both Houses in a vote on the address. Most Commonwealth Constitutions provide for an inquiry of a judicial nature before removal proceedings can be instituted, some requiring the advice of the Judicial Committee of the Privy Council. Our own method would be improved if we substituted for an address from both Houses as the only or alternative method, the advice of the Judicial Committee in all cases, and specified the grounds as misconduct or physical or mental inability. Actual removal following this advice would be by the Queen in Council, whereas it is doubtful at present what the appropriate instrument for removal would be.

The tenure of judges of inferior Courts is on a different basis. County Court judges are removable by the Lord Chancellor for inability or misbehaviour, and have a retiring age of 72 under the County Courts Acts. Recorders and chairmen of Quarter Sessions are similarly removable by the Lord Chancellor under various statutes. In practice they are as free from interference by the Executive or Parliament as the judges of superior Courts. Justices of the Peace in England may be removed from the commission of the peace by the Lord Chancellor or the Chancellor of the Duchy of Lancaster, if he thinks fit, although it is established practice not to remove them except for good cause. Under the Justices of the Peace Act 1949 a Justice of the Peace may also be placed on the Supplemental List (in effect, relieved of the more strictly judicial functions) on the ground of age or infirmity or other like cause or if he declines or neglects his judicial functions, and his name must now be placed on that List when he reaches the age of 70.

A Judicial Services Commission is contained in most recent Commonwealth Constitutions. The Commission is composed mainly of judges or retired judges with the Chief Justice as chairman, to give mandatory advice on the appointment of superior judges (except the Chief Justice), and the appointment, promotion and dismissal of inferior judges. The establishment of a Judicial Services Commission in this country would probably be desirable. There may well be no political risk attached to the advice of the Lord Chancellor, but it would be safer and look better if choice by the Executive were confined to the highest judicial post, as well as giving relief to the overburdened Lord Chancellor. A Judicial Services Commission would also be an advantage if solicitors became eligible for a wider range of judicial appointments, as the Lord Chancellor would not know so much about the qualifications of members of that profession as he does about the leaders of the Bar.

At the time of the economic crisis in 1931 an Order in Council was made under the National Economy Act authorising the Treasury to reduce the salaries of 'persons in His Majesty's service', and the Treasury were so tactless as to apply the cut to judges' salaries. Although the judges personally were willing to make the same financial sacrifices as other people, objection was taken to the method adopted on the ground that judges are not properly regarded as servants of the Crown. They are appointed and are dismissible by the Crown, but they are not subject to the orders of the Crown as to how they should carry out their duties. Bracton, Fortescue and Coke could be cited—against Bacon—to the effect that the judges enforce the law even against the King. If Parliament had intended the Act to apply to judges, they should have been specifically mentioned. The Treasury restored the cuts soon afterwards.

INDEPENDENCE OF THE JUDICIARY IN RELATION TO PARLIAMENT

The Houses of Parliament do not seek to interfere in the administration of justice. It is a Parliamentary custom that questions should not be asked in the House about the conduct of the Courts in particular cases. Also, the holders of judicial office (other than lay magistrates) are disqualified by statute from sitting in the House of Commons on the ground that they should not take part in political and party controversy.

OUR AMORPHOUS CONSTITUTION

In this discussion of the Courts and the Constitution we ought to recall that there is no judicial review of Acts of Parliament, as distinct from delegated legislation. No Act of Parliament can be declared 'unconstitutional' or void as being beyond the powers of Parliament to make, whether it increases the powers of the Executive or restricts the rights of the citizen or affects the tenure of the judicial office.

This proposition should be considered together with the fact that the House of Lords as the highest Court in the land no longer holds itself bound by its own precedents. In *London Street Tramways Co.* v. *London County Council* (1898) the House of Lords was asked to reconsider two of its previous decisions which had induced the Court of Appeal to decide against the appellants; but Lord Halsbury, Lord Chancellor, in the course of his judgment said that 'a decision of this House once given upon a point of law is conclusive upon this House afterwards, and . . . it is impossible to raise that question again as if it were *res integra*, and could be re-argued, and so the House be asked to reverse its own decision'. He admitted that a bad decision, if irreversible, might cause hardship in later cases, but it was in the interest of the State that there should be an end to litigation at some time. If the law ought to be changed, it can be done by legislation. A good deal of criticism of this doctrine was heard in later years from both practising and academic lawyers, and it was pointed out a few years ago that when an Israeli statute released the Supreme Court of Israel from the binding force of its own previous decisions, the House of Lords remained the only highest Court in the civilised world that regarded itself as bound by its own precedents. Not only did the Judicial Committee of the Privy Council occasionally depart from its own precedents in appropriate cases, but reference was constantly made to the relative freedom with which the Supreme Court of the United States regarded precedent.

Then one day in 1966 Lord Gardiner, the Lord Chancellor, made a Practice Statement on behalf of himself and the Lords of Appeal in Ordinary, in the course of which he said: 'Their Lordships . . . recognise that too rigid adherence to precedent may lead to injustice in a particular case and also unduly restrict the proper development of the law. They propose, therefore, to modify their present practice and, while treating former decisions of this House as normally binding, to depart from a previous decision when it appears right to do so.' He added that their Lordships would, on the other hand, bear in mind the danger of disturbing retrospectively the basis on which contracts, settlements of property and fiscal arrangements have been entered into and also the especial need for certainty in criminal law. The method chosen for announcing this *volte-face* was somewhat surprising, as it is difficult to see how an extra-judicial utterance can reverse a principle contained in an actual decision of the highest Court. Yet it would have been illogical to purport to reverse that principle in the course of a judicial decision, as the later decision would have had no greater weight than the *London Street Tramways Case.* It would have been better to pass a short Act of Parliament.

The Practice Statement was acclaimed both in the legal profession and among the academics, but amid the general satisfaction it was overlooked that the analogy to Courts like the American Supreme Court was unsound, because such Courts start from a written Constitution, and however far they seem to wander in the maze of interpretation it is to a written Constitution they return. Moreover, many foreign countries also have codified systems of law. We for our part have no written Constitution, and much of our criminal law and private law is not codified. In the past we have relied overmuch on judicial lawmaking. Now we find that our system, based on an unwritten Constitution and the absence of judicial review of legislation, and having at its apex a Court that has repudiated the binding force of precedent, is a flimsy superstructure on uncertain foundations, a fragile building erected on shifting sands.

6

The Individual and the State

NO STRICTLY 'FUNDAMENTAL' RIGHTS

The British Constitution contains no 'fundamental' rights in the strict sense. The principles relating to individual liberty can be altered by ordinary Act of Parliament, and there is no legal limit to the extent to which Parliament can abridge or abolish rights which in many Constitutions are regarded as fundamental. Jurisprudentially most of them are 'liberties' rather than rights. They are the residue of freedom allowed by law, the remnant left over when all the restrictions imposed by common law, Acts of Parliament and local by-laws have been subtracted. The doctrine of individual liberty itself is a common-law doctrine, and the older limitations are common-law doctrine resting on the accident of litigation; but added to these are a number of statutory restrictions or prohibitions imposed from time to time to meet some real or supposed public need.

No legal system allows, or could allow, *absolute* rights. All liberties must be restricted by the interests both of the State and of other individuals. There must be a balance of interests between the individual and the community. 'The safeguard of British liberty', as Lord Wright said in *Liveridge* v. *Anderson* (1942), 'is in the good sense of the people and in the system of representative and responsible government which has been evolved.' The practical checks are the influence of public opinion, the vigilance of the Opposition, and the restrictive interpretation placed by the Courts on legislation limiting individual freedom. Although we often speak of rights of the 'subject' or the 'citizen', for most purposes they are the same for aliens or citizens of other Commonwealth countries who are lawfully here as they are for citizens of the United Kingdom.

English law has much to be proud of, and little to be ashamed of, in pioneering the development and protection of civil liberties. Instead of merely formulating rights in the abstract, it has always emphasised the importance of enforcement by means of adequate remedies.

PERSONAL LIBERTY

The first and most important example is personal liberty. Every imprisonment, arrest or other kind of physical coercion is *prima facie* unlawful, and it is for the person imprisoning, arresting or otherwise coercing to justify his act in either civil or criminal proceedings if called upon to do so. There are a number of grounds for justification, such as arrest and detention pending trial on a specific charge of crime, or conviction and sentence for a specific offence after trial by a Court of competent jurisdiction, or custody pending extradition or deportation, or committal for contempt of Court or Parliament. If the deprivation of liberty is wrongful there are various legal remedies appropriate to different circumstances, including application for *habeas corpus*, appeal against conviction or sentence to a higher Court, a civil action for damages for assault, false imprisonment or malicious prosecution, a criminal prosecution for assault, or an application for a declaration as to the rights of the parties or for certiorari to have an order quashed. The common law allows a person to use a reasonable amount of force in defence of himself and his household, and this right of self-defence extends to resisting unlawful arrest without warrant, whether by a police constable or a private citizen; though it is inadvisable to resist arrest by a constable (as distinct from pursuing a remedy afterwards) since the arrest may well turn out to be lawful and then one will have committed the additional offence of resisting a lawful arrest.

The most efficacious remedy—an invention of the English common law—is the writ of *habeas corpus*, for which the person restrained or his legal adviser or anyone else on his behalf applies to the High Court by affidavit (sworn statement). If there is a *prima facie* case of unlawful detention, the Court will order the gaoler or other person concerned to state the reason for the detention and to show cause why the person detained should not be released. The Court, if satisfied after hearing argument that the detention is unlawful, will order the prisoner's immediate release. In vacation or at any time when a judge is not sitting in Court, such as at weekends or at night, application may be made to a judge sitting otherwise than in Court, for example, in Chambers, or in an emergency, anywhere. Thus in the *Soblen* case (1962), where the Home Secretary had made a deportation order that Soblen, an American citizen who had illegally entered this country, should be put on an aircraft bound for the United States, application was made to the Chambers Judge at his home in the middle of the night, and the Judge signed the order on his dining-room table. The remedy of *habeas corpus* cannot be suspended except by Act of Parliament, which is not in practice done in this country, though it has been done from time to time in Ireland during the Union, and the remedy is not available against the Executive by an alien enemy interned in wartime.

Although personal liberty is protected against everyone from the Sovereign or Home Secretary downwards, it is specially relevant to consider it in relation to the powers of the police. In *Christie* v. *Leachinsky* (1947) two police officers were held liable for false imprisonment because in arresting the plaintiff without a warrant and detaining him overnight they misinformed him of the nature of the charge; the true ground for the arrest would have required a warrant. A few years ago an engaged couple received more than £5,000 damages against two police constables for malicious prosecution and false imprisonment. On the other hand it was decided in *Fisher* v. *Oldham Corporation* (1930) that at common law the local police authority could not be made liable vicariously for torts committed by police officers in exercising their powers of arrest and detention because, although the police authority appointed and paid them, it did not control the manner in which they carried out their duties. And although constables are sworn to maintain the Queen's peace, the Crown could not be made vicariously liable either at common law or after the passing of the Crown Proceedings Act. The Police Act 1964 now provides that the Chief Constable is liable to be sued for torts committed by constables under his direction and control in the performance or purported performance of their functions in the same way as a master is liable for the torts of his servants. Damages and costs are payable out of the local police fund.

If a constable suspects a person of having committed a crime and wants to question him, he should arrest him for a specific reason and inform him of it. Otherwise there is no obligation to give one's name and address to the police or to answer their questions, still less to accompany them to the police station to help them with their inquiries. Of course, a law-abiding citizen will usually be willing to help the police in this way; but if a person is not willing, he has a defence to a charge of wilfully obstructing a police constable in the execution of his duty, and he might also have a claim for damages against the constable for false imprisonment and perhaps assault. The law relating to search is not very clear, but it seems that a constable may search a person whom he has arrested, and take property found in his possesion that would provide evidence at the trial of his having committed the crime for which he was arrested.

There are some offences for which a constable may make an arrest without a warrant, notably breaches of the peace in his presence and wilful obstruction of the highway, and also where the constable reasonably suspects that the prisoner has committed an 'arrestable' offence (formerly called a 'felony'). Otherwise the constable must obtain a warrant, that is, a written authorisation, signed by a Justice of the Peace after hearing a sworn statement, for the arrest of a named person. In less serious offences a summons to appear in Court is usually issued, a warrant for arrest being applied for if the person summoned fails to appear.

The practice of police questioning is regulated by the Judges' Rules which, though not rules of law, are rules the non-observance of which may lead the Court to reject statements by the accused as evidence against him. They are designed especially to prevent the extortion of admissions or confessions by threats or offers of reward. In requiring repeated 'cautions' they lean over backwards in favour of suspected persons, and although on the one hand they discourage third degree methods, on the other they often make the detection of crime unnecessarily difficult. The main rules are that a police officer, as soon as he has evidence for reasonably suspecting that a person has committed an offence must, before asking him further questions, 'caution' him that he is not obliged to say anything unless he wishes to do so, but that anything he says may be put into writing and be given in evidence at his trial; that when a person has been formally charged questions are strictly limited and he must be cautioned again; and that a confession will not be admitted in evidence unless the prosecution is able to prove that it was not obtained by fear of prejudice or hope of advantage. A witness of some incident is also free to decline to make statements to the police or to answer their questions: in that event he can be served with a *subpoena* by the Court, ordering him under a penalty to come to the Court to give evidence in proceedings.

English law does not countenance preventive detention, or detention for more than a strictly limited period before trial. (The Northern Ireland Special Powers Act 1922 is an exception, which was originally intended to be temporary and to remain in force only from year to year but was extended indefinitely in 1933). A person who has been charged with an offence may not be kept in custody by the police for more than twenty-four hours without being brought before a magistrate; if that is not practicable, the station officer may release him on bail. The grant of bail pending trial is usually done by magistrates, who have a discretion whether to grant it in the more serious crimes. The chief considerations are whether he is likely to abscond, and whether he is likely to commit further offences if he is set free. The gravity of the charge is relevant to both. If a person committed for trial at Assizes or Quarter Sessions is refused bail, he may apply to the High Court. The Bill of Rights provides that bail shall not be 'excessive', and by modern statutes appeal lies to a judge in chambers against the amount of bail. There are also provisions for the grant of bail pending an appeal.

The ancient power of magistrates to 'bind over' is anomalous. Where a breach of the peace or offence against public order is threatened or apprehended, a person may be required to enter into a bond (called a 'recognisance') to keep the peace or to be of good behaviour, so that if he commits a breach of the order during the stated period he and his sureties (if any) may forfeit the amount in which they are bound. The anomaly is that if the defendant refuses to enter into recognisances, or is unable to find the necessary sureties, the Magistrates may send him to prison for a period not exceeding six months or until he sooner complies with the order, even though he may not yet have been convicted of any offence. This appears to be an exception to the proposition that there is no preventive detention in English law, but committal to prison can be avoided if the defendant is willing to be bound over, provided he can find the sureties who may be required. There is now an appeal against a binding-over order.

FREEDOM OF SPEECH

Freedom of speech similarly is the liberty to express one's opinions orally, in writing or in print, provided that the law is not infringed. It is associated with freedom of conscience and of worship, and also the right to receive information and ideas through any medium. Among the most important constitutional aspects are the freedom to express and propagate political views, including criticism of the Government, and the associated freedom of the press; freedom of debate in Parliament; the immunity of judges, counsel, witnesses and jury taking part in judicial proceedings; and the privilege of publishing fair and accurate reports of Parliamentary debates and judicial proceedings. The law is infringed by such offences as treason, seditious libel, provoking public disorder, breaches of the Official Secret Acts, incitement of the armed or police forces to mutiny or disaffection, obscenity, and contempt of Court; by the tort of libel or slander; and by contempt of Parliament. There is in English law no 'censorship' in the sense of requiring the *prior* approval of any official to the publication of any matter. The Licensing Acts requiring a licence to print expired in 1695, and the censorship of modern stage plays instituted by an Act of 1843 was abolished in 1968.

Since Fox's Libel Act 1792 declared and enacted that in a prosecution for criminal libel the jury may give a general verdict of 'Guilty' or 'Not Guilty', and may not be directed by the Court to find the defendant guilty merely on proof of the publication by him of matter which the judge rules is seditious, prosecutions for seditious libel became far less common, and after the time of the Reform Act 1832 a charge of seditious libel ceased to be a political weapon. The intention necessary for the offence is an intention to bring into hatred or contempt, or to excite disaffection against the person of the Sovereign, or the Government and Constitution, or either House of Parliament or the administration of justice, or to excite people to attempt, otherwise than by lawful means, the alteration of the law, or to raise discontent or disaffection among the people, or to promote feelings of illwill and hostility between different classes of people. It is not seditious, on the other hand, to show that the Government has been mistaken, or to point out defects in the Constitution, or to excite people to attempt by lawful means the alteration of the law, or to point out (with a view to their removal) matters that produce feelings of hatred or illwill between classes of people. Prosecutions for seditious libel are rare nowadays, and are not instituted in practice unless there is incitement to violence. In *R.* v. *Caunt* (1947) a newspaper proprietor was prosecuted for writing an anti-Semitic article in terms that could scarcely fail to promote feelings of illwill and hostility between groups, but Mr. Justice Birkett told the jury it must be proved that the accused published the libel with the intention of promoting violence, and they acquitted.

The civil law of defamation, especially libel (written or printed matter), is a great defence for the individual, who may protect his reputation against untrue defamatory statements by an action for libel and an injunction to restrain their further publication. Journalists and others who make a living by their pen are constantly attacking the strictness of our law of libel; but we ought to be very careful before we allow a whittling down of this shield of the defenceless and unorganised against a professional and organised minority who have a vested interest in being allowed to publish anything they think makes a 'story'. The Defamation Act 1952 did make a reasonable reform in allowing an 'offer of amends', that is, an offer to publish a suitable correction and apology, which if accepted stays the action, and if not accepted entitles the defendant to prove that he had no intention to refer to the plaintiff.

The freedom of the press, said Chief Justice Mansfield in the celebrated *Dean of St. Asaph's Case* (1783), consists in 'printing without any previous licence, subject to the consequences of law'. He was following Blackstone's *Commentaries*, first published in 1765, where it is stated that the liberty of the press 'consists in laying no *previous* restraints upon publication, and not in freedom from censure for criminal matter when published'. Hamilton in 1804 described the liberty of the press as 'the right to publish with impunity, truth, with good motives, for justifiable ends though reflecting on government, magistracy or individuals'. The 'press' generally covers printed matter of all kinds, and not merely newspapers. Newspapers enjoy a few minor concessions in recognition of the fact that they have often to be produced under pressure and with little time for correction; but the general principle is that there is no *special* freedom of the press. Certainly there is no licence for journalists to obtain information by methods that would be wrongful in the ordinary person as by trespass, nuisance or otherwise. Nor have journalists the privilege to refuse to disclose the sources of their information when called on as witnesses in judicial proceedings or statutory inquiries. So when three journalists refused to answer relevant and essential questions about the sources of their information at the Vassall Tribunal of Inquiry in 1963, they were sentenced to short terms of imprisonment. The Court will not in practice insist on an answer if it does not consider the information essential to the case.

The Official Secrets Acts have come in for a good deal of criticism. The basis of the present law is an Act which passed through all its stages in the House of Commons within twenty-four hours in the hot summer of 1911. This Act makes it a criminal offence 'for any purpose prejudicial to the safety or interest of the State' to approach any prohibited place, to make sketches or plans that may be useful to an enemy, or to communicate to any other person any sketch, document or information that may be useful to an enemy. In *Chandler* v. *Director of Public Prosecutions* (1964), where members of the Committee of 100 were charged with entering an R.A.F. station, the House of Lords held that the question whether the purpose of the accused–namely, to sit in front of aircraft so as to prevent them from taking off–was 'prejudicial to the safety or interests of the State' was a question for the Court after hearing evidence from the Crown as to what were the interests of the Government, and not a question for the jury on which the accused could give evidence as to their ultimate object, which was to bring about nuclear disarmament, which they considered would be beneficial to this country. This decision appears to have been a new departure. But the main criticism of the Official Secrets Acts is the allegation that they are used to prevent or punish the passing on of information that could not usually be said to affect the national security. So it has been suggested that it ought to be a good defence to a prosecution under the Acts to show that neither the national interest nor legitimate private interests were likely to be harmed, and that the information was passed and received in good faith and in the public interest.

The law relating to contempt of court has also come in for a good deal of criticism. Its main purpose is to discourage activities interfering or likely to interfere with the fair conduct of a trial. Thus it is contempt of Court to publish comments on a pending case which are calculated to interfere with the course of justice by prejudicing a fair trial. The law of contempt in this country stands in the way of pre-trial by the press, radio or television; whereas in the United States the press takes part in the detection of crimes, reports interviews with suspects and witnesses, comments on the course of judicial proceedings and expresses opinions on whether suspects are guilty. Insults to the judge in Court or the publication of scurrilous abuse of a judge with reference to his judicial conduct, are contempt of Court; but not genuine criticism of his judicial conduct, made in good faith and not imputing improper motives. 'Justice is not a cloistered virtue,' in Lord Atkin's well-known aphorism: 'she must be allowed to suffer the scrutiny and respectful, though not outspoken, comments of ordinary men.'

A major criticism of the law was met by the Administration of Justice Act 1960, which provided that it should be a defence to show that at the time of publication the accused, having taken all reasonable care, did not know and had no reason to suspect that proceedings were pending. Other criticisms were met by provisions of the same Act abolishing attachment for contempt and requiring an order of committal to be made in open Court, and allowing an appeal from a committal order to a higher Court.

The statutory offence of obscenity is hardly of constitutional importance. The subject has aroused a great deal of discussion because it is to the interest of writers and the producers of plays and films to be free from restrictions, and the most profitable freedom is that which follows after the abolition of a previous restriction. How far, if at all, the law ought to try to uphold moral standards in the arts, or to what extent we want to have for the first time in history a completely permissive society, are controversial questions; but the difficulty of applying the Obscene Publications Acts in particular cases is not of itself a sufficient reason for doing away with all restrictions, for the Courts constantly have to deal with more complex problems.

ASSOCIATION; PUBLIC MEETINGS, PROCESSIONS AND DEMONSTRATIONS

The rights of association and assembly similarly consist in the liberty of two or more persons to associate or meet together, provided they do not infringe any particular rule of law, either by having an unlawful object or by adopting unlawful means. The freedom to form political parties is the most important constitutional aspect of the right of association, though the latter also includes the formation of trade unions. Public meetings and processions have engaged the attention of Parliament and the Courts from time to time over the years. It is curious to recall that quite recently they were regarded as having lost their importance owing to the development of television discussions and broadcast talks, for since then we have witnessed demonstrations for nuclear disarmament, peace campaigns and other more ephemeral objectives.

At common law, as Dicey said, the right of public meeting was the result of the view taken by the Courts as to *individual* liberty of person and speech. If A may go where he likes so long as he does not trespass, and say what he likes to B so long as it is not defamatory or seditious, and if B, C and D etc. may do the same, we arrive at a general 'right'. The limitations, even at common law, are quite extensive, including as they do trespass, nuisance, sedition, riot and unlawful assembly. The importance of trespass here is that all land is owned by someone, and local authorities are generally the owners of parks and open spaces in towns and of the surface of highways (most public roads, streets and squares). As the right of using the highway is that of 'passing and repassing', with such reasonable extensions as looking at shop windows, there cannot be a right to hold a stationary meeting on the highway without the licence of the owner, usually the local authority – apart from the fact that a meeting on the highway is very likely to cause an obstruction. Parks and open spaces are intended for the recreation of the general public, and their use is regulated by local by-laws. So, again, permission is commonly required to hold meetings there. Parks and open spaces in London, notably Trafalgar Square and Hyde Park (a royal park), are regulated under various statutes by the Minister of Public Building and Works, who consults the Home Secretary and the Commissioner of Metropolitan Police before granting permission to hold meetings there (usually confined to Saturday afternoons, Sundays and bank holidays). It would be more appropriate if they were put under the control of the Home Secretary. Local authorities may hire out their premises for a reasonable fee, and they must do so to Parliamentary candidates holding election meetings. It has been suggested that they should be required to provide premises for hire to any organisations that applied for them; but this surely would be quite impracticable: there is no limit to the number of bodies that might compete for this facility.

Some of the decisions on common law offences, such as unlawful assembly (the gist of which is a breach of the peace, whether actual, threatened or apprehended), are unsatisfactory, being *extempore* judgments of a Divisional Court given at a time when there was no further appeal. In the celebrated case of *Beatty* v. *Gillbanks* (1882) it was held that officers of the Salvation Army had been wrongly held guilty of unlawful assembly merely because they persisted, in spite of a Justice's notice and a police direction, in holding their processions and meetings in Weston-super-Mare knowing that a rival organisation called the 'Skeleton Army' systematically opposed them, with the result that considerable disturbance occurred. That case was actually an appeal against a binding-over order. A charge of unlawful assembly is not often brought nowadays, as the police prefer to bring a charge of wilfully obstructing a constable in the execution of his duty. This statutory charge, made triable summarily in 1885, was intended to be used defensively, but the charge is now often used offensively, as it were, in order to stop meetings where a breach of the peace is feared. The Executive have no power to *prevent* the holding of meetings, though the police may order a meeting to disperse without waiting for a breach of the peace if they have reason to believe that a breach of the peace will take place and that there is no other way of avoiding it.

The statutory offences that may be committed by those taking part in a public meeting include disorderly conduct, threatening, abusive or insulting words and behaviour, obstructing the highway, malicious damage to property, assaulting or obstructing a police officer in the execution of his duty, wearing political uniforms and carrying offensive weapons. Special provisions apply to London. Thus not more than ten persons may carry a petition to the Houses of Parliament, and not more than fifty persons may assemble to consider or prepare a petition within one mile of Westminster Hall or the Law Courts while Parliament or the Courts are sitting. The Commissioner of Metropolitan Police has special powers to prevent the obstruction of streets in the metropolis. The famous Riot Act 1714 was recently repealed along with the distinction between felonies and misdemeanours, but the common law offence of riot (the gist of which is a violent and tumultuous disturbance of the peace) remains.

One has also to bear in mind local by-laws. By-laws may require Council or police permission to be obtained before a meeting or procession is held in a public place, and they may forbid the distribution of pamphlets in order to prevent litter. Breach of a by-law is a summary offence.

Processions are in a somewhat different category. Being meetings on the move, as it were, processions on the highway are not *prima facie* a trespass, and they are perhaps less likely to constitute an obstruction. In *R.* v. *Clark* (1964) the Court of Criminal Appeal quashed a conviction for inciting persons to commit a nuisance by obstructing the highway after taking part in a demonstration during a visit of Greek royalty, on the ground that a procession is lawful if there is a reasonable use of the highway even though the highway is temporarily obstructed. On the other hand the Public Order Act 1936, passed in a period of Communist and Fascist processions in London, provides that a chief police officer, if he reasonably thinks that a procession may cause serious public disorder, may prescribe the route it shall take; and if he thinks this power is insufficient he may apply to the local Council for an order prohibiting the holding of all or any class of public processions in his area for a period not exceeding three months. The Council may then, with the consent of the Home Secretary, make such order. A similar order may be made in London, where the Police Commissioner goes straight to the Home Secretary for his consent. The three months' period may, with the Home Secretary's consent, be extended for a further three months, by which time experience shows that rival factions have cooled down.

It follows from what has been said that there is, strictly speaking, no *right* to 'demonstrate' in a public place: there is freedom to demonstrate if one avoids committing specific breaches of law. In practice, the restraint in controlling crowds shown by sorely tried police (who would be better employed catching burglars or having a weekend rest), and the exercise of discretion not to prosecute many minor offences, allow a useful safety-valve to the emotions of those who feel strongly about certain questions, for it must be candidly admitted that part of the purpose of demonstrating lies in baiting the police and committing minor breaches of the law in order to draw attention to strongly-held minority opinions.

It has been objected that the traditional approach to this branch of the law puts an exaggerated emphasis on trespass, and that the law is or should be capable of changing with the times, which require rights (in the strict sense) to hold public meetings and demonstrations; but the critics have failed to make out a case for saying that in English law there either are or should be rights (in the strict sense) to do these things *in a public place* as distinct from private premises. This does not necessarily mean, as has been said before, that such meetings or demonstrations are unlawful, still less that prosecutions will be brought in all cases.

English law does not discriminate between persons except on such reasonable grounds as alienage, immature years or mental condition. On the other hand the common law did not forbid discrimination against classes of persons by members of the public. The Race Relations Act 1965, which created the offence of incitement of racial hatred by means of written matter or words in a public place or at a public meeting, was yet another example of *ad hoc* legislation. It was of doubtful necessity as the matter was covered by the law of sedition, at least where there was incitement to violence; and the Public Order Acts covered writing or speech intended or likely to cause a breach of the peace. But it was also the purpose of the 1965 Act, which was extended in 1968, to prevent racial discrimination of certain kinds by providing for investigation and conciliation by a Race Relations Board and local Conciliation Committees, with the ultimate sanction of civil proceedings in the County Court. The objections to the creation of the offence of incitement of racial hatred are, first, that it is not necessary to show that any public disorder was caused, and secondly that by legislating against specific kinds of discrimination, namely, 'colour, race or ethnic or national origins', Parliament might be taken to imply that other grounds of discrimination, such as religious beliefs or political opinions, are legitimate.

RIGHT OF PROPERTY

Private property is protected by the law relating to such crimes as theft, malicious damage and forcible entry, and such torts as trespass, nuisance and conversion. A magistrate's search warrant, granted on sworn information, is required at common law for entry on private premises, except that a constable may enter without a warrant in order to prevent the commission of an arrestable offence (formerly a 'felony'), to prevent or suppress a breach of the peace or to recapture someone who has escaped from lawful arrest. Statutes creating criminal offences also sometimes allow entry on private premises under warrant for the purposes of the Act. There are strictly limited exceptions where entry and search may be made by a constable under the authority of a senior police officer in the case of stolen goods, explosives and official secrets.

No taxation, central or local, is lawful except under an Act of Parliament. The compulsory acquisition of the ownership or possession of land or goods by a government department or local authority for public purposes, such as defence, roads, housing, schools or hospitals, also requires the authority of an Act of Parliament. The statute always provides for compensation and the method of assessing it. The right to fair compensation would be one of those set out in a new Bill of Rights if we had one. The use and development of land are now regulated by Planning Acts, and the letting of houses by Rent Acts. Many questions arising out of this legislation are decided by special tribunals, most of which are under the general supervision of the Council on Tribunals, though there is generally an appeal to the High Court on a question of law.

EMERGENCY POWERS OF THE EXECUTIVE

The preservation of public order, or 'the Queen's Peace', is a prerogative right and duty of the Crown. Before the development of professional police forces under nineteenth-century legislation, the maintenance of order rested mainly on sheriffs, mayors and magistrates; now it is primarily the responsibility of the police acting under statutory powers and their common-law powers as constables. They are not armed, except in rare cases of extreme danger. Every citizen has the duty to assist a police constable to suppress a breach of the peace if reasonably called upon to do so, though prosecutions for refusing assistance are very rare. The Home Secretary is the Minister ultimately responsible in England. Any degree of force, even the destruction of life or property, may be used if necessary to suppress riot or insurrection, but the degree of force must be proportionate to the necessity. The assistance of the military should be invoked only as a last expedient. A soldier for the purpose of establishing civil order, it has been said, 'is only a citizen armed in a particular manner.' If troops are ordered to fire, the civil and military authorities responsible will be legally answerable for death, personal injury or damage to property caused by any use of force that was not reasonably necessary in the circumstances. The Petitition of Right 1628 condemned martial law in time of peace, and the better opinion is that 'martial law', in the sense of the suspension of the ordinary law and the substitution of discretionary government through the military, or anything like a Continental 'state of siege', is unknown to our constitutional law.

In modern times Governments have to arm themselves with statutory powers to meet all the administrative problems raised by emergencies in war or peace. The Defence of the Realm Acts in the first war, and the Emergency Powers (Defence) Acts in the last war gave extremely wide powers to the Executive, covering every aspect of the national defence and economy. No more striking examples of Parliamentary supremacy can be shown than these last. The Act of 1939 gave a general power by Order in

Council to issue such Regulations as appeared to the Government 'to be necessary or expedient for securing the public safety, the defence of the realm, the maintenance of public order and the efficient prosecution of any war in which His Majesty may be engaged, and for maintaining supplies and services essential to the life of the community'; and an Act of 1940 (which was passed through all its stages in both Houses and received the Royal assent in one day) simply allowed Defence Regulations to make provision 'for requiring persons to place themselves, their services, and their property at the disposal of His Majesty'.

Permanent provision in peacetime is made by the Emergency Powers Act 1920, under which a state of emergency may be declared by royal proclamation if it appears likely that the community will be deprived of the essentials of life by interference with the supply and distribution of food, water, fuel, light or transport. Parliament is to be informed, and if necessary summoned. Regulations, to be laid before Parliament, may confer on Ministers the necessary powers for dealing with the emergency; but no Regulations may impose military or industrial conscription, alter the rules of criminal procedure, or illegalise strikes or peaceful picketing. Proclamations have been issued under the Act at times of serious dock, transport or power strikes, and on a few occasions Regulations have been made. The Emergency Powers Act 1964 authorises the temporary employment of members of the armed forces in agricultural work or other urgent work of national importance. The Special Powers Act in Northern Ireland has already been mentioned.

PARLIAMENTARY COMMISSIONER ('OMBUDSMAN')

A Parliamentary Commissioner, popularly known as the 'Ombudsman' after his Scandinavian prototypes, was established by Act of Parliament in 1967 to investigate and report on complaints of maladministration against government departments. He is not concerned with breaches of law for which remedies lie in the Courts, nor with the exercise of discretionary powers, nor with policy. His concern is with complaints by private citizens that they have suffered injustice by reason of a government department's failure to observe proper standards of administration. Mr. Crossman, when the office was created, suggested that maladministration would cover bias, neglect, inattention, perversity and turpitude. An example would be the Crichel Down case (1954) where a landowner complained that the Ministry of Agriculture had refused to return to him after the war part of his land that had been requisitioned during the war and was no longer required by the Ministry for the purpose for which it had been requisitioned, but which the Ministry wished to retain as a model farm. Before 1967 the citizen's only remedies were for his member of Parliament to ask a question in the House, to raise the matter in debate on the Adjournment or on Supply, to correspond with the Minister or ask him to hold an inquiry.

The Parliamentary Commissioner is appointed by the Crown, and his tenure of office is similar to that of a Supreme Court judge. He must make an annual report to Parliament. Because of our strong tradition of Ministerial responsibility, complaints may only be referred to him through a member of Parliament. The new institution is therefore a supplement to, and not a substitute for, the work of the backbencher. The functions of the Commissioner overlap those of the Council on Tribunals, of which he is a member. The Commissioner has power to call for oral or written evidence and to compel the production of documents, including departmental minutes, but excluding Cabinet papers. He has a discretion to refuse to take up a case where he thinks it is outside his terms of reference or there are insufficient grounds for the complaint. If he finds nothing wrong, he informs the member who approached him. If he finds there was good reason for the complaint and the department agrees to put it right, he will inform the member; otherwise he may report his conclusion to Parliament. A Select Committee of the House of Commons considers the Commissioner's reports. It also deals with complaints from members who think that the Commissioner has failed to deal properly with cases forwarded by them, and it may recommend changes in the law; but it does not interfere with the working of the Commissioner or act as a court of appeal from his findings. Following the experience in Scandinavia and New Zealand, it is found that in most of the cases investigated the administration is exonerated. About 10 per cent of the complaints investigated are upheld, the greater number being cases of unjustifiable delay.

In the first eighteen months just over half of the cases referred to the Commissioner were rejected as being beyond his terms of reference, which appear to be either too narrow or too narrowly construed. Maladministration has since been extended to include bad decisions where the departmental procedure for reviewing a rule, or the grounds for maintaining it, are defective; but the Commissioner in his review for 1968 said that the extension of his review to cover the quality of decisions had made little difference in practice, and he had not so far come across any decision indicating bias or perversity. Other criticisms would be met by the establishment of a system for investigating complaints of maladministration in local government, which would involve independent reports for consideration by the appropriate local authority; the appointment of a Health Commissioner, which would involve consultation with the medical profession; and the appointment by the Home Secretary of a Judge Advocate of Police or an independent person to represent the public in the investigation of complaints against the police. Reform is also needed to cover the Public Corporations administering nationalised industries and services, including the Post Office. A few local authorities have already appointed an official to hear complaints against them and to report.

UNIVERSAL DECLARATION AND EUROPEAN CONVENTION

The Universal Declaration of Human Rights adopted by the General Assembly of the United Nations in 1948 was drafted in very wide terms and imposed merely a moral obligation on the members to see that their law was in line with it. The European Convention for the Protection of Human Rights and Fundamental Freedoms of 1950 obliges the signatories, including the United Kingdom, to guarantee to all persons within their jurisdiction certain rights and freedoms. These are drafted in greater detail than the Universal Declaration, specifying the chief exceptions and limitations, and there is a partly adoptive enforcement machinery through the European Commission of Human Rights, the Committee of Ministers of the Council of Europe and the European Court of Human Rights. The United Kingdom by an executive act in 1966 accepted the compulsory jurisdiction of the European Court, and recognised the right of individuals to bring petitions against her before the European Commission, which can adjudge the United Kingdom liable to afford 'just satisfaction' to the injured party. However, the Convention is not incorporated into British constitutional law. It is binding on the United Kingdom morally and in international law, but as a matter of British constitutional law there is no obligation on Parliament to bring English law into line with the Convention.

The formulation of the 'Rule of Law' in the Declaration of Delhi, 1959, includes among the minimum standards or principles for the law those contained in the Universal Declaration and the European Convention, mentioning in particular freedom of religious belief, assembly and association, and the absence of retroactive penal laws; and in relation to the criminal process it states that a 'fair trial' involves such elements as certainty of the criminal law, the presumption of innocence, reasonable rules relating to arrest, accusation and detention pending trial, the giving of notice and provision for legal advice, public trial, right of appeal, and absence of cruel or unusual punishments.

Our law on the whole stands up well to these tests, which is not surprising since the eighteenth-century concept of natural rights, from which the modern concepts of fundamental and human rights have been developed, was based largely on what Blackstone called the general rights of Englishmen. The principle that there should be at least one right of appeal, however, did not extend to the refusal of *habeas corpus* in criminal cases or to committal to prison for contempt of Court, but in these respects English law was reformed by the Administration of Justice Act 1960.

The biggest gap in this part of our legal system is that a general right of 'privacy' is not recognised as it is, for example, in more than half of the American States. The law of trespass, nuisance and defamation go a good deal of the way, but they do not cover the whole ground. Protection is inadequate against unscrupulous methods of collecting news for the press; the commercial exploitation of another's personality, as by misappropriating his name or photograph; the use of computerised information for a purpose different from that for which it was collected; and the unreasonable infliction of noise, as by piped music and the ubiquitous transistor radio. Further threats come from technological advances and extensions of the means of communication, such as telescopic lenses, bugging devices, and lie detectors in job interviews.

The right to leave one's country, mentioned in the Universal Declaration, is infringed in so far as passports are issued or refused by virtue of the prerogative and remain the property of the Crown, so that they may be impounded or withdrawn. Instances of this, however, are actually very few, and the effect, strictly, is to make it difficult or impossible to enter another country rather than to leave this one.

Recognition by Ministers of Education of the article in the Universal Declaration that 'parents have a prior right to choose the kind of education that shall be given to their children' is becoming extremely tenuous.

The European Declaration condemns discrimination in the enjoyment of rights 'on any ground such as sex, race, colour, language, religion, political or other opinion, national or social origin, association with a national minority, property, birth or other status', so it is unfortunate that a recent British statute should pick out one example, incitement to racial hatred, for the creation of a criminal offence.

It is questionable whether, in the absence of a criminal code, the Courts ought to be able to create offences, such as that of public mischief. A person making false statements to the police and thereby wasting their time on useless investigations has been held guilty of a public mischief, though it has since been stated that a conspiracy is necessary. There are several cases where the Court has convicted of conspiracy to effect a public mischief (by distribution on the home market of pottery intended by statutory order for export), or conspiracy to corrupt public morals (the *Ladies' Directory Case*). The enactment of a Criminal Code would make such judicial lawmaking unnecessary.

On the other hand, everyone has duties to the community as well as rights. Indeed, there has been an over-emphasis on rights in recent years. The exercise of rights, states the Universal Declaration, may be limited by law for the purpose of securing due recognition and respect for the rights of others and of meeting the just requirements of morality, public order and the general welfare in a democratic society; and the European Convention follows the Universal Declaration in negativing the right of any State, group or person to engage in any activity aimed at the destruction of any of the rights set forth therein.

OUGHT WE TO HAVE A NEW BILL OF RIGHTS?

In order to prevent the gradual erosion of individual liberties, many modern Constitutions incorporate a Declaration of Rights. Most post-war Constitutions of Commonwealth countries include such a Delcaration, with power of judicial review. The first was the Indian Constitution of 1950, in which the fundamental rights and their qualifications, based partly on the American Bill of Rights and partly on English constitutional experience, are elaborated in considerable detail. The Nigerian declaration of fundamental rights of 1960 provided a model for later formulations in other Commonwealth countries. The ratification by the United Kingdom of the European Convention, and the acceptance of the jurisdiction of the European Court, are also relevant here.

CANADIAN AND NEW ZEALAND EXPERIENCE

The Attorney-General of New Zealand (Mr. J. R. Hanan) introduced a Bill of Rights into the House of Representatives in 1963, based on the Canadian Bill of Rights and the Universal Declaration, but it was rejected by a select Constitutional Reform Committee. Introducing the Bill the Attorney-General said it would be of value to formulate clearly and concisely the rights and liberties of the people; the balance between the individual and the State had over a long period been moving in the direction of the State, and the time had come to reassert the fundamental liberties of the citizen. Many in this country today are beginning to share Mr. Hanan's view. The introduction of a Bill of Rights, argued the Constitutional Society of New Zealand in support, draws the attention of Parliament and people to the study of the freedom of the individual in the modern State, his rights as a human being and his duties to his neighbour. The concepts found in a Bill of Rights are usually expressed as generalities, the words used are necessarily abstract, and the Bill is pervaded by general principles and declaratory statements. It is intended, however, not only to direct the Courts on matters of interpretation, but even more as something to be read, understood and remembered by the people. It would provide a standard by which the people could judge the actions of the Government of the day. There is the educational value of enunciating in a general way a set of principles by which people may be guided. But a Bill of Rights is no substitute for a written Constitution protected by a bicameral Legislature, which is what the Constitutional Society itself was advocating.

There are two methods by which a Bill of Rights might be enacted. One is the method adopted by the Canadian Bill of Rights of 1960. This declared in broad terms the main existing individual rights, but did not impose legal limitations on the law-making power of the Canadian Parliament—which, like the British Parliament, is incapable of binding future Parliaments; but it directed the Courts to construe and apply every existing or future Act of the Canadian Parliament in conformity therewith, unless it was expressly declared that it should operate notwithstanding the Bill of Rights. This was an ordinary statute of the Federal Parliament which had no special constitutional status, and could be amended or repealed at any time by ordinary legislation. It has had little practical effect on litigation: Canadian appellate Courts have treated it as providing rules of construction and have been unwilling to declare Federal legislation void. Its main importance, in the opinion of Mr. Justice Bora Laskin, the Canadian constitutional expert, may lie in the direction to the Minister of Justice to examine all proposed legislation for consistency with the purposes and provisions of the Bill of Rights and to report any inconsistency to the House of Commons.

The other method, which it is submitted is the only one worth all the trouble involved, is to *entrench* a declaration of rights as part of a written Constitution with judicial review. Mr. Lester Pearson, when Prime Minister of Canada, proposed to introduce an entrenched Charter of Human Rights in a new written Canadian Constitution. The needs of the people, he said, take priority over the needs of government. A primary purpose of government, as Locke wrote, is to secure basic freedoms; but agreement on common values would be an empty gesture unless they are given special legal protection. Mr. Lester Pearson's draft Charter was adopted by his successor, Mr. Trudeau, in 1969.

The Canadian and New Zealand Parliaments, like the United Kingdom Parliament, are incapable of binding themselves in future or their successors. Hence, when it was desired to introduce a Bill of Rights it was done in Canada–and attempted in New Zealand–by the 'Interpretation Act' method. Revision of the whole Canadian Constitution, which is the British North America Act 1867 as amended, has provided the opportunity of including an *entrenched* declaration of fundamental rights. It was also in connection with a proposal to enact a written Constitution for New Zealand that discussion has taken place in that country for an entrenched declaration of fundamental rights. Meanwhile the New Zealand Electoral Act 1956, s. 189, discussed in the next chapter, incorporates certain reserved provisions.

It is almost certainly not possible for a Bill of Rights to be effectively entrenched in our law, except as part of a written Constitution containing entrenched clauses, with judicial review, because Parliament cannot bind its successors. This becomes part of the wider question discussed in the next chapter.

7

Conclusion: Need for a Written Constitution

CONSTITUTION AT THE MERCY OF PARTY MAJORITY
IN THE COMMONS

The British Constitution is found to be largely at the mercy of a small, temporary party majority in the House of Commons. We have seen that this situation has arisen as a result of unplanned historical development. Why has it been allowed to remain? Because it has suited the leaders of both sides in the political 'game', giving inordinate power to the Prime Minister of the day, which will be inherited by the Leader of the Opposition in due course, while the general public are apathetic or unaware.

Each of our previous chapters–dealing with the Constitution generally, the Government, Parliament and both its Houses, the Courts, and individual liberties–has led to the conclusion that a written Constitution with judicial review is desirable for this country. We have seen that there are no legal limits to what Parliament can do by ordinary legislation, that the Government virtually controls the activities of Parliament, that the maximum duration of a Parliament is too long, that the existence of a (reformed) Second Chamber with some power of rejection or delay is essential, that important areas of law and practice are uncertain, that the 'Parliament Act 1949' is of doubtful force, that too much power is concentrated in the hands of the Prime Minister, that the dissolution of Parliament needs to be regulated, that the law relating to judicial tenure should be improved, and that there is a call for a new Bill of Rights. In our system, or lack of system, all exists on sufferance, depending on the legislative supremacy of Parliament. There are permanent, or at least abiding, principles of constitutional government in the national interest as against the sectional interest of a temporary and perhaps small party majority; but the former can only be secured against the latter by limiting the power of Parliament, which in effect means placing restrictions on the Government of the day.

PURPOSE OF ENACTING A CONSTITUTION

The purpose of enacting a Constitution – the institutional laws, the main conventions relating to the Executive, and the fundamental individual rights – would be partly to clarify the principles, but mainly to entrench the most important provisions against repeal or amendment except by some specially prescribed procedure. At present it is possible for constitutional changes to be brought about by a majority of one in the elected Chamber. A Government elected with a small majority may not be truly representative of the people after its first year of office. The strength of party discipline means that the Government controls the Legislature. Restrictions on the Legislature would therefore in practice be restrictions on the Government. In the recent proposals of the Canadian Government for a new written Constitution it was argued that the mechanism for ensuring democratic government should be the subject of constitutional guarantees, and that the institutions of government and individual rights are fundamental to the whole Constitution.

The function of a written Constitution, then, would be to entrench the main institutions of government, the relations among themselves and between them and the private citizen. Foremost among these provisions – apart from matters on which there has been no conflict since 1688, such as the Monarchy and succession to the throne, and taxation – would be the following:—

National rights of England, Scotland, Northern Ireland and Wales as members of the Union.

Regional rights, if there is a further measure of devolution.

The status of the Channel Islands and the Isle of Man.

The Second Chamber, its composition and numbers, and its powers in relation to legislation. Disputes between the two Houses might be settled differently according to whether the matter was general Government policy, such as economic policy, or Fundamental Rights.

Provisions relating to Parliamentary government, in particular, the reduction in the maximum life of Parliament to four (or perhaps three) years; annual meeting of Parliament; and Electoral laws, including Boundary Commissions.

Common Market membership and obligations (if we join).

Formulation of certain constitutional conventions, to protect the Queen as ultimate guardian of the Constitution as far as possible from involvement in politics, and to reduce the power of the Prime Minister. Such formulations would include the choice of Prime Minister, and the dissolution of Parliament, when and by whom advised.

The appointment, tenure and independence of the Judiciary–a reformed judicial tenure, substituting the advice of the Judicial Committee of the Privy Council for an address from both Houses in the removal of Judges, and perhaps establishing a Judicial Services Commission.

A new Bill of Rights, preserving notably *habeas corpus* and the free expression of opinion, and taking account of the European Convention.

Emergency powers and their limits; entrenchment to prevent government by decree or the establishment of extreme one-party rule.

The Constitution would be declared to be the supreme law of the land. Jurisdiction in constitutional questions (judicial review) would be conferred on the superior Courts, with appeal to the Judicial Committee of the Privy Council or a Special Constitutional Court.

Procedure for constitutional amendment, e.g. a two-thirds majority in each House for a Bill describing itself as a Constitutional Amendment Bill.

A written Constitution in itself would not clear up uncertainties in the law; indeed, a cynic might argue that it would increase them; but the exercise of drafting one would provide a unique opportunity for a wide and thorough overhaul of both the laws and the conventions. Further, its enactment–even apart from entrenchment sanctioned by judicial review–would fit in with our current phase of codifying various branches of English law, in particular, the proposal for a Criminal Code.

ARGUMENTS AGAINST A WRITTEN CONSTITUTION WITH JUDICIAL REVIEW

The general arguments used by lawyers against the adoption by this country of a written Constitution with judicial review are that it would lead to rigidity, that it would increase the volume of litigation, and that interpretation of the Constitution would involve the Courts in the decision of political questions. Rigidity, however, is a matter of degree, depending on the method prescribed for constitutional amendment. It need not be excessive, nor need the enactment of a Constitution prevent the growth of new conventions. In a unitary State or Union it is unlikely that there would be a great increase in litigation. Nor is it likely that many of the questions of construction that came before the Courts would be policy questions. The main objection hitherto has arisen from the innate conservatism of the common lawyer, his attachment to judge-made law and his dislike of statute law. He is not accustomed to a category of cases called 'constitutional'.

With regard to constitutional conventions there are legitimate queries. Are some of the conventions sufficiently definite to be capable of formulation in a statute? Are there some conventions that it would be undesirable to crystallise in statutory form? Are the Courts a suitable forum for adjudicating upon the proper observance of conventions? It is undoubtedly difficult to formulate conventions, though in a number of the newer Commonwealth Constitutions it has been attempted. They have incorporated the most important conventions relating to the exercise of governmental powers, either specifically or by reference to the British practice. The kind of problem that may arise is illustrated by the case of *Adegbenro* v. *Akintola* (1963). Under the 1960 Constitution of the Western Region of Nigeria the Governor had power to dismiss the Premier if it appeared to him that the Premier no longer commanded the support of a majority of members of the House of Assembly. The Governor dismissed the Premier, Chief Akintola, on the strength of a letter signed by a majority of members of the House, and appointed Adegbenro in his place. A political emergency arose during which the matter was taken to the Courts. The majority of the Federal Supreme Court of Nigeria, following what they understood to be the constitutional convention in Britain, held that the dismissal of Chief Akintola was invalid, as the Governor's power to dismiss the Premier was exercisable only when the House of Assembly itself had formally signified its lack of confidence in him. This decision was reversed on appeal by the Judicial Committee of the Privy Council, who came to the conclusion that the Governor was entitled to obtain his information as to whether the Premier had lost the confidence of the House from any apparently reliable source. A somewhat similar case arose in Sarawak in 1966 with the opposite result, when the High Court of Malaysia in Borneo held that the Governor of Sarawak (if he had power to dismiss his Chief Minister) could dismiss him only following the unfavourable vote of the Legislature, and that a letter of no confidence was insufficient. In each country a constitutional amendment later nullified the judicial decision.

Factors to be taken into consideration are that the making of declarations by the Court is discretionary; that the Courts are reluctant to make decisions that will be ineffective; and that matters of this kind, such as whether a Prime Minister ought to resign or whether the Head of State may dismiss him, are usually decided by political methods and procedures, depending ultimately on public opinion. Lord Radcliffe, in the Privy Council case cited, referred to the lack of judicially discoverable and manageable standards for resolving such disputes, and thought that Courts were hardly suitable bodies to answer such questions.

We would not propose the formulation of constitutional conventions except as part of the exercise of enacting the Constitution as a whole, although the conventions relating to the exercise of the powers of the Governor-General of New Zealand did have to be formulated without enacting the rest of that country's Constitution as it appeared that his Letters-Patent needed to be redrafted. On the other hand, if we find it desirable on other grounds to enact a Constitution we could not leave out the Executive altogether, while to incorporate the laws relating to the Executive without referring to the conventions would be equally impracticable. Mr. Trudeau thinks that in the new Canadian Constitution conventions should be formulated in a general way, and his draft includes outline provisions relating to the government and covering the Head of State, the Executive, the Privy Council, the Prime Minister, the Cabinet, and the Ministers. The solution to this problem may be to provide that such existing conventions as are enacted shall not be justiciable. We have some rules that are expressly non-justiciable, for example, the functions of the Speaker under the Parliament Acts. It has been held by the Court of Appeal of New Zealand in *Simpson* v. *Attorney-General* (1955) that the Governor-General's statutory obligation to issue writs for a general election is not justiciable. Although the Courts may find in such cases that the exercise of statutory discretions is impliedly not justiciable, it would be preferable in the Executive part of the proposed Constitution to specify any particular provisions that are to be non-justiciable.

RIGHTS OF THE INDIVIDUAL

The first problem in framing a declaration of rights is that of selection. Most of the 'rights' of the individual that would be contained in a declaration of rights would be liberties, involving restrictions on the Legislature and enforceable against members of the Executive, such as personal liberty, freedom of speech, association, assembly and worship. In some instances, for example, non-discrimination, there might be redress against private persons. Some, such as the franchise, would be political in the strict sense. This and a few others would be available to citizens only: most would be available to all persons lawfully present in this country. The inclusion of general duties of the State or Government to provide welfare benefits, education, health services and so on, is not suggested. Such economic or social rights find a place in some Constitutions as 'Directive Principles of State (or Social) Policy', and are expressly declared to be not judicially enforceable. They are rather ideals or guides to Legislatures and Governments, and at most might have some slight effect on the construction of ambiguous statutes.

The next major problem is that of drafting. One has to consider in each case both the proposition and the exceptions. Should the language be general like the American Bill of Rights, or should it be detailed, specifying the various limitations and exceptions like the Fundamental Rights in the Indian or Nigerian Constitution? On the one hand, the First Amendment to the United States Constitution provides simply that 'Congress shall make no law . . . abridging the freedom of speech or of the press', an impossibly general statement that has caused endless difficulty for the Supreme Court. On the other hand, section 24 of the Federal Constitution of Nigeria (1960) read as follows: '(1) Every person shall be entitled to freedom of expression, including freedom to hold opinions and to receive and impart ideas and information without interference. (2) Nothing in this section shall invalidate any law that is reasonably justifiable in a democratic society– (a) in the interest of defence, public safety, public order, public morality or public health; (b) for the purpose of protecting the rights, reputations and freedom of other persons, preventing the disclosure of information received in confidence, maintaining the authority and independence of the courts or regulating telephony, wireless broadcasting, television, or the exhibition of cinematograph films; or (c) imposing restrictions upon persons holding office under the Crown, members of the armed forces of the Crown or members of a police force.' Expressions like 'reasonably justifiable' and 'democratic society' would provide many pitfalls for judges faced with the task of construing them; but prominence would rightly be given to 'protecting the rights, reputations and freedom of other persons' at a time of increasing licence on the part of the press, and growing intolerance on the part of noisy minorities who try to break up meetings held by speakers with whose opinions (if they listen to them) they do not agree.

Critics of a Bill of Rights raise the question, what would be the effect on existing legislation? The exceptions, they argue, might nullify the propositions. The Constitution would have to state, if that is the intention, that the declaration of Rights was not to have retrospective effect, though it would raise presumptions of interpretation. But if no change in the existing law is intended, why go through the trials and tribulations of drafting a Bill of Rights? As far as criminal or civil liability is concerned, the principle would remain that people may do what they like unless forbidden by law. Some changes might be made in the existing law, such as the recognition or extension of the right of privacy. What would be the effect of a declaration of the invalidity of a subsequent statute on those who have *bona fide* acted under it? There would be uncertainty and much litigation, it is said, and the Courts would be required to decide policy questions. These questions reveal fears that in this country might well prove unfounded. The answer may lie partly in the device of prospective overruling, which is discussed later.

CAN PARLIAMENT BIND ITSELF?

'If an Act of Parliament had a clause in it that it should never be repealed', said Chief Justice Herbert in the celebrated case of *Godden* v. *Hales* (1686), 'yet without question, the same power that made it may repeal it.' The proposition that Parliament cannot bind itself or its successors appears to some people to express a paradox. If there is something Parliament cannot do, they ask, how can we speak of its legislative supremacy? But the paradox is verbal only. If the proposition is put in the form, 'Parliament is not bound by its predecessors', the difficulty vanishes. There is no judicial authority for the power of *express* repeal or amendment: it is so well established that it has not been raised in the Courts. If Parliament intends to repeal or amend a previous statute it usually does so expressly; but through oversight this may not be done, in which case the Courts will try to reconcile the two statutes as far as they reasonably can. Otherwise, a later Act or section supersedes an earlier Act or section with which it is inconsistent; in other words, it impliedly repeals or amends the earlier. So in *Ellen Street Estates Ltd.* v. *Minister of Health* (1934), where there was a discrepancy in the methods of assessing compensation prescribed by the Acquisition of Land (Assessment of Compensation) Act 1919 and the Housing Acts 1925 and 1930, the Court of Appeal held that the Housing Acts impliedly repealed the Act of 1919 in so far as they were inconsistent. 'If in a subsequent Act', said Lord Justice Maugham, 'Parliament chooses to make it plain that the earlier statute is being to some extent repealed, effect must be given to that intention just because it is the will of the Legislature.'

Special considerations may apply, as we mentioned in chapter I, where the earlier Act is part of an arrangement of an international character, such as the Statute of Westminster, Independence Acts and perhaps the Act of Union with Scotland, though even there it is likely that British Courts would regard themselves as bound by the later Act, regardless of any political or international repercussions.

The advocacy by the Constitutional Society of New Zealand of a written and entrenched Constitution for that country, including a Bill of Rights, has not so far been successful. Meanwhile the New Zealand Legislature, suffering perhaps from a guilty conscience in having abolished the Second Chamber in 1950 and been unable to devise a substitute, included in the revised Electoral Act of 1956 a section (s. 189) stating that certain provisions relating to such matters as the life of Parliament (consisting now only of the House of Representatives and the Governor-General), the franchise and secret ballot, should not be repealed or amended except by a majority of 75 per cent of all the members of the House or by a simple majority of votes at a referendum. Section 189 was not itself one of the provisions requiring this special procedure for repeal or amendment. There are three views as to the effect of a provision such as this. The first is that it is binding on the Legislature as providing a new definition of 'Parliament' for this particular purpose: this is an adoption of the 'manner and form' argument discussed below. The second view is that the special amending procedure could be evaded, but that it would have to be done in two stages: the New Zealand Parliament could (and would need to) repeal section 189 first, and then it could proceed to amend the reserved provisions. This seems to be rather a pointless technical distinction, as the two things could be done in two consecutive sections of the same statute. The third view, which we think is the correct one, is that section 189 constitutes merely a moral sanction, albeit a strong moral sanction amounting to a constitutional convention. The reason why the Legislature did not try to 'entrench' section 189 itself is that it appreciated that a double pseudo-entrenchment would be no stronger than a single pseudo-entrenchment, and so *ad infinitum*. As Bacon said in his *Maxims of the Law:* 'Acts which are in their nature revocable, cannot by strength of words be fixed or perpetuated'.

Jurists tell us that there must be some 'rules of recognition' (Hart) or 'rules of competence' (Alf Ross) by which we may know what Parliament is and what is an Act of Parliament. From this some constitutional writers draw the conclusion that Parliament can bind itself as to the *manner and form* of legislation, and that therefore if it prescribed a special procedure for the alteration of particular laws, such as electoral laws or fundamental rights, the Courts would not uphold amendments to such laws unless they were made by the special procedure laid down. They follow the late Sir Ivor Jennings in citing the case of *Attorney-General for New South Wales* v. *Trethowan* (1932), in which the Judicial Committee of the Privy Council held that the New South Wales Legislature had no power by a statute passed in 1930 (after a change of Government) to abolish the Second Chamber without a referendum, because that Legislature had passed an Act in 1929 providing that the abolition of the Second Chamber would require approval at a referendum. But the reason for that decision was that the State of New South Wales was subject to the Colonial Laws Validity Act 1865, which declared that a representative colonial Legislature had wide powers of lawmaking so long as its laws did not conflict with statutes of the United Kingdom Parliament applying thereto, and provided that its laws were passed 'in such manner and form as may from time to time be required' by any law (including a Colonial law) for the time being in force in the territory. Clearly the decision was based on the fact that the New South Wales Legislature was a *subordinate* legislature, bound by the 'higher law' laid down by the United Kingdom Parliament. The analogy from a subordinate to an autonomous Legislature is false.

Then they cite the famous 'Cape Coloured Voters case' (*Harris v. Minister of the Interior*, or *Harris v. Dönges*, 1952), in which the Appellate Division of the Supreme Court of South Africa rightly held invalid a statute passed by the South African Parliament purporting to place the Cape coloured voters on a separate electoral roll, because it had not been passed in accordance with the special procedure (a two-thirds majority in both Houses sitting together) prescribed for this kind of constitutional amendment by section 152 of the South Africa Act 1909. Now the South Africa Act was the Constitution of South Africa, which created the South African Parliament itself. But because it happened for historical reasons to be an Act of the United Kingdom Parliament and South Africa had since the Statute of Westminster 1931 been recognised as an independent sovereign State, there was a good deal of confusion between State sovereignty and the 'sovereignty' of Parliament, although it was pointed out that Congress is limited by the American Constitution but no one would deny that the United States is a sovereign State. Partly to avoid the supposed difficulty of ascribing limits to a 'sovereign' Parliament, an ingenious formula propounded by Professor D. V. Cowen was adopted, which involved a quibble with the word 'Parliament'. Although for general purposes the bicameral 'Parliament' of South Africa was sovereign, the 'Parliament' for the purpose of amending section 152 of the South Africa Act was a two-thirds majority of a unicameral body. *Dicta* were thrown out to the effect that a similar line of reasoning might be applied to the United Kingdom Parliament, which could thus bind itself. Again, the *Harris* case is a false analogy, for the South African Parliament was bound by a higher law, namely, the South African Constitution.

The same applies to two recent appeals in the Privy Council

from Ceylon. In *Bribery Commissioner* v. *Ranasinghe* (1965) it was held that the Bribery Tribunal by which the respondent had been convicted was not lawfully appointed; and in *Liyanage* v. *R.* (1967) it was held that a court of three Judges (without a jury) nominated for the particular case, by which the accused were convicted of offences arising out of an abortive *coup d'état*, was not lawfully appointed. In both cases the reason for the decision was that the statute under which the tribunal or Court was set up involved a constitutional amendment requiring a special legislative procedure which had not been complied with. Ceylon is an independent sovereign State by virtue of the Ceylon Independence Act 1947, but its Legislature is bound by a higher law, the Constitution of Ceylon, which is contained in an Order in Council of 1946.

One cannot be dogmatic on this matter, but the view put forward here is that a legislature cannot bind itself, whether as to subject-matter or the manner and form of legislation, unless it is authorised (directed or empowered) to do so by some 'higher law', that is, by some prior law *not laid down by itself*. Our test is the probable attitude of the Courts. Suppose Parliament passed an Act this year providing that the voting age should not be raised except with the approval of a majority of 75 per cent in the House of Commons. It is submitted that if Parliament passed another Act next year raising the voting age and approved by a bare majority in the House of Commons, British Courts would not hold the second Act void. As Lord Pearce said in *Bribery Commissioner* v. *Ranasinghe*, lawmaking powers in all countries with written Constitutions must be exercised in accordance with the terms of the Constitution from which the power is derived. His Lordship added that any analogy to the unwritten British Constitution 'must be very indirect, and provides no helpful guidance'. The reason why the New South Wales Legislature in *Trethowan's* case had to follow the procedure of a referendum prescribed by its own previous statute, was that it was directed to do so by the Colonial Laws Validity Act 1865 ('in such manner and form as may from time to time be required by any Act of Parliament, Letters Patent,

Order in Council, or *Colonial Law* for the time being in force in the said Colony').

If there must be some rule logically prior to Parliament by which an act can be recognised as an Act of Parliament, this identifies Parliament: it does not limit its powers. Since the early middle ages (except during the revolutionary Commonwealth period in the seventeenth century) 'Parliament' has meant the Sovereign, the Lords and Commons in Parliament assembled. An Act assented to by the Queen by and with the consent of the Lords and Commons in Parliament assembled could abolish the monarchy or the House of Lords. P1 would not have bound itself as to the laws it can pass: it would have been replaced by P2. But to say that the prescription of some special legislative procedure for certain Bills is to alter the meaning of 'Parliament' for those purposes is a play upon words.

It would probably not be effective to try to *prevent* the passing of a Bill that infringed an enactment corresponding to the Canadian Bill of Rights or section 189 of the New Zealand Electoral Act. The case of *Harper* v. *Home Secretary* (1955), where an injunction was refused to restrain the Home Secretary from presenting a draft Order (approved by both Houses) relating to electoral boundaries to Her Majesty in Council, is an illustration of the unwillingness of the British Courts in our present system to interfere with the Parliamentary process, apart from the fact that by the Crown Proceedings Act no injunction (as distinct from a declaration of private rights) may be issued against a Minister in his official capacity.

HOW A NEW BRITISH CONSTITUTION MIGHT BE ENTRENCHED

The solution is to bring into being a 'New' Parliament which would owe its existence to a Constitution *not enacted by itself*, from which it would derive both its powers and its limitations. When the possibility of Great Britain and Ireland forming a federation with a rigid Constitution was discussed in the 1880s, Bryce expressed the opinion that Parliament could extinguish itself and a new Federal Legislature could be established following this *breach of continuity*. Then the new Constitution could only be altered in accordance with its own terms. Dicey thought Parliament could *transfer* its powers to another Legislature, but it seems that the *extinction* of the existing or 'Old' Parliament and the creation of a new Parliament would be the more effective method. A Constitution limiting the powers of the 'New' Parliament, in the manner suggested earlier in this chapter, would be adopted by the 'Old' Parliament, and then submitted for adoption by the people in a referendum. The Old (unlimited) Parliament would be abolished, and it would be superseded by the New (limited) Parliament.

Alternatively, it might be preferable for Parliament first to transfer its powers to a *Constituent Assembly*, and at the same time to abolish itself. The Constituent Assembly would then draft a Constitution creating a Parliament with limited powers. Again, the New Parliament would have only such powers as the Constitution gave it. That raises the question of how the Constituent Assembly would be appointed. In some countries the existing Legislature has functioned as a Constituent Assembly, but we can hardly envisage the present Parliament acting in this capacity until the composition of the House of Lords has been reformed. It is probable that a specially appointed Constituent Assembly, if one could be devised, would be the most influential.

The statute adopting the Constitution, or setting up the Constituent Assembly, as well as the Constitution itself, would require the Judges (existing as well as future) to take an oath of loyalty to the new Constitution.

We have suggested that the new Constitution should be submitted for adoption by the people at a referendum. This is because the establishment of a new Constitution is the most solemn and fundamental of all constitutional acts: its approval at a referendum, by putting the new Constitution in a special category, would confer on it the highest possible prestige. Elsewhere in this book we have expressed objections to the general or frequent use of the referendum as a constitutional process, and we do not suggest that this 'unEnglish' device should be employed for subsequent constitutional amendments. Our proposal is for an initial or fundamental referendum only.

CONSTITUTIONAL AMENDMENT

The argument from inflexibility would be largely met, first, by ensuring that all provisions of the Constitution would be amendable in one way or another, and, secondly, by providing that entrenchment need not be total. There would be no parts of the Constitution like the basic articles of the Cyprus Constitution or (according to the recent *Golak Nath Case*) the fundamental rights in the Indian Constitution, that could not be amended at all. Some special procedure for amendment would be required for such parts as the Monarchy, the Unions with Scotland and Northern Ireland, the Islands, the Regions, the Second Chamber, the life and frequency of Parliament, the franchise, the Boundary Commissions, judicial tenure, fundamental rights, emergency powers, judicial review of legislation, and the procedure for constitutional amendment itself. Parts that need not be entrenched, but could be amended by the ordinary legislative procedure, could include details such as the number of seats in the House of Commons, and non-justiciable provisions covering what are now conventions.

An Amendment Bill should be so specified, for this draws the attention of members of Parliament and the public to its significance. The Lord Chancellor or Minister of Justice would be required to examine all Bills with reference to their compatibility with the Constitution and to report. In difficult cases an advisory opinion could be sought from the Judicial Committee of the Privy Council under the Judicial Committee Act 1833, which provides that the Crown may refer any question of law to the Committee for an advisory opinion. The opinion of the Judicial Committee may already be required on the validity of legislation of the Northern Ireland Parliament under the Government of Ireland Act 1920. This procedure would not be appropriate, however, if the Judicial Committee were to be given jurisdiction to decide cases arising out of the interpretation of the Constitution.

CONCLUSION

A referendum, we have already suggested, would not be desirable as part of the process of constitutional amendment. It is difficult to frame a complex technical question in a way suitable to be answered 'yes' or 'no' by large numbers of people who have not the necessary background and have not followed all the previous discussions. A joint sitting of the two Houses is a doubtful device, at least until we know what sort of Second Chamber we shall have and how its members will be chosen. The most satisfactory method for amending the entrenched clauses would therefore appear to be a Constitution Amendment Bill passed by a special majority of (say) two-thirds in each House. It would be necessary to state whether this was to be a two-thirds majority of members present and voting, or two-thirds of all the members of each House.

JUDICIAL REVIEW OF LEGISLATION

Judicial review, as we saw in chapter 1, is the traditional method of testing the validity of legislation in the United States and Commonwealth countries. A body of judicial precedents of constitutional interpretation is then gradually built up. Certain provisions could, as we have said, be expressly made non-justiciable, such as those relating to the Sovereign's exercise of the prerogative, the functions of the Speaker in the House, and existing conventions relating to the Cabinet system. It would not be necessary for the judges themselves to invent, as the American Supreme Court has done, a loosely defined class of 'political questions' which are not suitable for judicial decision.

The objection that difficulty would be created where acts have been *bona fide* performed under legislation later declared void by the Courts might be met, at least in some cases, by the doctrine of 'prospective invalidation' or (where a precedent of interpretation is being reversed) 'prospective overruling'. This means that the Court could declare, in cases where it thought there were compelling reasons for doing so, that the statute concerned would be invalid in future, but without prejudice to things *bona fide* done in reliance on it down to the time of the judgment. This device has been occasionally used by the American Supreme Court during the last forty years. Thus, previous cases having decided that the conviction of a person on the strength of evidence seized by the police in a manner contrary to the Constitution was void, the question arose in *Linkletter* v. *Walker* (1965) whether all prisoners convicted on evidence unlawfully obtained ought to be released and retried. The Supreme Court held that this drastic action was not necessary, but that the Court could deliver judgment with prospective effect. Again, in *Golak Nath* v. *State of Punjab* (1967) the Indian Supreme Court holding (probably wrongly) that the Indian Parliament had no power to amend any of the fundamental rights declared in the Constitution, even by the special amending process, overruled previous decisions of its own over a number of years upholding several amendments to the fundamental rights: but having regard to the history of the amendments (relating to such matters as agrarian reform), their impact on the social and economic affairs of the country and the chaotic situation that might be brought about by the sudden withdrawal of the constitutional amendments at that stage, the Court, borrowing the idea from its American counterpart, confined the operation of the decision to the future. On the other hand, the doctrine of 'prospective' overruling or invalidation has met with criticism from both American and Indian lawyers as being a repudiation of the principle that the function of judicial review is to declare unconstitutional laws to be *void*; that Courts which invalidate laws for the future are acting as legislators altering the law, although the Constitution is supposed to be supreme.

Ultimate appellate jurisdiction would be conferred by the new Constitution on some Court in any cases in which a constitutional issue is raised. Some countries have special Constitutional Courts with exclusive jurisdiction in constitutional cases, but it would be preferable for us to integrate this jurisdiction with the general jurisdiction of the superior Courts. Constitutional questions could then be dealt with in the normal course of litigation, and in relation to other legal questions that are usually involved in such cases. The House of Lords in its judicial capacity, being technically part of the Legislature, would not be an appropriate appellate Court for this purpose. This points to the Judicial Committee of the Privy Council as the most suitable choice. It already hears appeals from some Courts and tribunals in this country as well as from Courts overseas, and the judicial strength of these two bodies is much the same. It could hardly be objected that the Judicial Committee is in form a committee of the Executive.

The choice of the Judicial Committee would also fit in with the prospect that, as a result of a radical reform of the Second Chamber, the Judicial Committee might become the ultimate court of appeal for *all* kinds of cases, an idea that has been mooted from time to time during the last hundred years.

MORAL AND EDUCATIONAL VALUE OF A WRITTEN CONSTITUTION

Finally, there is the moral and educational value of introducing a written Constitution enunciating in a systematic and inspiring way a set of principles by which people may be guided, and embodying the concepts of legality, stability and permanent values. It is not valid to compare the United Kingdom with other countries that have written Constitutions entrenching fundamental rights and judicial review, and to point to the present political chaos in some of these countries and the plethora of judicial precedents in the United States. There are political and social factors at work in some of the new Commonwealth countries that fortunately do not obtain here, while the American judicial experience is largely due to the manner in which the American Federal Constitution was originally drafted at a time when judicial review seems not to have been intended, and also to the exceptional difficulty of amending that Constitution. In view of the law-abiding tradition and political maturity of this country on the one hand, and the relative flexibility of our proposed new Constitution on the other, the only valid comparison is between the present lack of system in this country and the situation it is hoped would obtain if we had a written Constitution of the kind suggested. In other words, the comparison is between the United Kingdom before and after.

It may be that the leading politicians of the two main parties would at first be hesitant to adopt such a basic and comprehensive reform. The essence of the British constitutional system has been described as two alternating and self-perpetuating oligarchies with supporting retinues, who are capable of collusion when it suits them. Many lawyers would be sceptical, having a romantic attachment to 'judge-made' law and a prejudice against legislation. The initiative for such an ambitious but worthwhile project is therefore likely to depend for its support on the formation of a sufficiently strong body of informed public opinion.